Schools in the Spotlight

T0333415

Pressure on schools to be publicly accountable for their policies and results has inevitably led to more institutions being thrust into the media spotlight. *Schools in the Spotlight* is a hands-on guide to understanding and improving your school's relationship with the media, helping to turn unwanted publicity into positive promotion. Issues covered include:

- Getting the right relationship with the media
- Managing public relations and writing press releases
- Coping with crisis and unwanted publicity
- Dealing with interviews
- Integrating media relations into whole school policy

This book also contains helpful case studies based on real life incidents, with discussions on possible solutions, and useful addresses and contacts are provided.

Governors, headteachers and everyone involved in schools management will find *Schools in the Spotlight* an essential guide to giving their school the best possible public image.

Tim McClellan is a journalist and a principal lecturer in corporate communication at Southampton Institute. **Nigel Gann** is a senior education consultant specializing in school improvement.

Schools in the Spotlight

A guide to media relations for
school governors and staff

Tim McClellan and Nigel Gann

London and New York

First published 2002
by RoutledgeFalmer
11 New Fetter Lane, London EC4P 4EE

Simultaneously published in the USA and Canada
by RoutledgeFalmer
29 West 35th Street, New York NY 10001

RoutledgeFalmer is an imprint of the Taylor & Francis Group

© 2002 Tim McClellan and Nigel Gann

Typeset in Sabon and Gill by BC Typesetting, Bristol
Printed and bound in Great Britain by
Biddles Ltd, Guildford and King's Lynn

British Library Cataloguing in Publication Data
A catalogue record for this book is available from the British Library

Library of Congress Cataloging in Publication Data
McClellan, Tim, 1957–
    Schools in the spotlight: a guide to media relations for school
governors and staff/Tim McClellan and Nigel Gann.
        p.   cm.
    Includes bibliographical references and index.
    ISBN 0–415–23061–6
    1. Schools–Public relations–Great Britain. 2. Community and
school–Great Britain. 3. Education in mass media.
I. Gann, Nigel, 1948– II. Title.

LB2847.M42 2002
659.2'9371'00941–dc21
                                                    2001031909

ISBN 0–415–23061–6

Contents

Chapter 1

Schools and the public

A historical context

How schools have dealt with and been affected by the media. How things might be better.

The Information Revolution

We know so much more now about what affects our lives in this country than we did only a few years ago. We can watch parliamentary debates on the television and listen to them on the radio. We can see politicians, civil servants and leading professionals being grilled by aggressive interviewers – a Home Secretary being asked the identical question seventeen times in succession. We can demand to see our medical records, read the ingredients on a packet of food, compare the different performances of schools, colleges and universities in public examinations. If all else fails (and if we have the time), we can search millions of websites on the Internet. And, of course, if we want other people to know what is happening to us, and what we think about it, we can publish it in just a matter of minutes.

This explosion of information has applied mainly to the public sector. It gives the public rights and, to those of us who serve the public, it gives responsibilities. It is part of a cycle in which increased knowledge leads to greater accountability, which in turn leads to greater access, which itself in turn makes more information available. Within the cycle, the two areas of activity with which this book concerns itself – schools and the media – are inextricably linked. Schools and media organizations need each other and feed off each other. They have more interests in common than areas of conflict. Yet they are often seen as being in conflict. Many schools still see it as a priority to 'keep out of the papers' – except for prize day and the opening of the new school library. A call from a local journalist as often as not sends the shutters up. A call from a national tabloid can induce panic.

In this chapter, by way of introducing the theme of the book, we trace some of the significant changes that have taken place in the public perception of schools since the information explosion began in the early 1970s. We do this for two reasons. First, we want to use the brief case studies to show those types of relationships with the media which have, and those which have not, been helpful in the past. Second, we want to look at the ways in which schools have been required to 'open up' about themselves.

Three schools in Islington

Between 1965 and 1975, three Inner London schools hit the local and national headlines. In all three, the 'presented problems' were lack of discipline and low standards. In at least two of the three, however, the approaches to discipline and teaching methods were quite deliberate policies introduced by the headteacher and staff of the time. How could they have failed so badly either to understand the impact their policies would have, or to 'sell' their ideas?

At Risinghill Comprehensive School in Islington, the headteacher's 'progressive' ideas fell foul of the politicians. Islington has been for some years a fashionable place for politicians and media people to live. Even if they did not send their own children to these schools, they would certainly know people who did. As the former George Orwell School discovered more recently, no school in Islington can hide its problems. At William Tyndale Junior School, it was the parents – at least some of them – who objected to the new head and deputy's style. In both these schools, it could be said, policies which might be – indeed, were – implemented quietly in hundreds of schools elsewhere in the country brought a school to its knees because staff were unable to persuade parents, local politicians and the media that their way of education worked. At the third school, it could be said, the senior staff had no deliberate policy: it just seemed that things were largely out of control. Once again, the case acquired a high profile because local (Labour Party) politicians were involved. But the school was not 'brought down'. Instead, a new senior management team reinstated an orthodox approach, and trouble was kept more or less under wraps. The school survived – the one example of the three where it could be argued that incompetence in the job, rather than in the management of relationships with the public and the media, was the weakness. How could this be, in establishments traditionally so impervious to public scrutiny and criticism?

The two worst schools in London?

'A school depends for a large part of its success on the confidence of parents' (Macpherson, 1972). So wrote a reporter for the London *Evening Standard* in its feature on a large North London secondary school in 1972. The article was the first in an 'occasional series' on London schools. The school featured in this opening salvo happened to be – statistically – one of the least popular in London. It had a history of self-perpetuating low achievement. Earlier in its life, as a secondary modern in scruffy Victorian premises, it had played second – perhaps third or fourth – fiddle to other schools in an area where, because of the density of the population, parents could relatively easily exercise choice if they knew how to go about it. Just down the road, the former grammar school could effectively select its intake through parent interview. The school was also suffering from the 'Risinghill effect'.

As Islington Green moved into its spanking new seven-storey premises in 1965, the Inner London Education Authority (ILEA) was closing down the nearest comprehensive after an unprecedented political campaign to which local and national newspapers had been recruited. Risinghill (see Berg, 1968), through its headteacher Michael Duane, had created a humane and supportive regime for children from one of the most disadvantaged parts of London. The aspect that gained most publicity was that the head refused to hit children, some of whom came from desperately poor, occasionally violent, backgrounds. With a perspective of thirty years, we can see now that Risinghill was just the first in a series of campaigns addressing, or playing on, the fears that parents have that schools might be running out of control.

By the time Islington Green was coming in for its (more than fair) share of newspaper coverage, seven years had passed since Risinghill had met its Armageddon. The ILEA's admissions system aimed at completely comprehensive intakes for its secondary schools. Children were tested at the age of 10, placed in one of five ability bands, and distributed among local schools. But parents could appeal against their child's placement. Few, though, appealed to have their child allocated to Islington Green. It takes many years for a community to stop talking about 'the grammar' and 'the secondary mod'. The parents who had taken their own grammar school education for granted, and who were able to provide a supportive home environment, expected to have access to a grammar school equivalent. Former grammar schools, by their own interview procedures and by parental selection, were by and large able to maintain high rates of exam success. Former secondary moderns were seen as perpetuating failure in results. The introduction of the Certificate of Secondary Education in 1965 tended to exacerbate this division. It was seen by some as a second-rate examination for second-rate schooling.

Meanwhile, other differences could be easily observed. Former grammar school comprehensives tended to enforce strict rules about uniform and out-of-school behaviour. Former secondary moderns often had a more relaxed approach to discipline. They lived with the consequences: 'One incident of violence in the playground and the news is buzzing round all the surrounding streets and takes a year or two to forget', wrote the London *Evening Standard* (ibid.). Islington Green had, staff were told in 1972, the highest number of assaults on staff by pupils of any school in London.

Such attitudes to schools could be reinforced by the media. Local papers often wrote of 'top schools' and 'sink schools'. When pupils at 'top' schools took drugs, thieved and rioted, newspapers were shocked at the disjunction between their behaviour and their environment. Reports tended to be of the 'man bites dog' variety. Such behaviour at a 'sink' school, however, was no cause for surprise. Rather, it reinforced the failure of the teachers, the parents, the local education authority, to alter the innate patterns of behaviour of 'problem' children.

In the case of Islington Green, the *Evening Standard* reported, 'Twenty top ability children were directed there – and the parents of all but six managed to get them sent somewhere else instead' (ibid.). The *Daily Telegraph* (1972) splashed the school's 'sink' status when the chair of governors refused to have her own child attend the school. As a leading member of the local Labour Party, she had perhaps more clout than most. That section of the press with a political agenda supporting the Conservative Party and opposed to the comprehensive system predictably had a field day with the hypocrisy of the egalitarian socialists.

Schools have always found it very difficult to change their reputation – their 'public image'. Judgements made about schools tend to focus on two pieces of evidence: the behaviour of the children, and the examination and test results. Schools can therefore easily get locked into an image that is self-perpetuating. Lazy journalists may look for incidents that confirm a public image of a school, just as they may look for, and report with relish, the predictable behaviour on an estate, or of a television star or a footballer.

Despite the appointment of fresh senior staff, the school continued to have public problems. Being in Islington within the eye of the media did not help. Fours years on, Peter Wilby reported, 'confidence is restored but difficulties remain'; 'Margaret Maden, like most comprehensive school heads, was chosen for her abilities as a manager and a projector of the school's external image. . . . Miss Maden has won over parents, primary heads, journalists, local authority officials. The really difficult task – welding the school into a common unit, working towards common aims – remains, as it must after so short a time, incomplete' (Wilby, 1976).

The media and educational reform

The power of the media to contribute to, if not actually bring about, political and legislative change was illustrated just a few years after the Islington Green saga. Since 1965 and throughout the 1970s, there had been a steady drip-drip of prejudice masquerading as public opinion about schools. The same themes predominated: standards and discipline. The Sutton Centre in Nottinghamshire, Countesthorpe College in Leicestershire, Madeley Court in Shropshire, Aberdeen's Summerhill School all suffered similar fates (see Fletcher *et al.*, 1985). Underneath the superficial shock-horror headlines lay a more pervasive theme: who owns our schools? Who decides what should happen in them? Before the 1960s, the answer to these questions was clear. It was the professional educationists – though local and national politicians might have some small influence.

The ownership of schools was much more obviously the battlefield in perhaps the most notorious educational media story of the century. The William Tyndale story contained the seeds of every subsequent piece of educational legislation between 1980 and 1997.

For the purposes of this book, the trials of William Tyndale Junior School in Islington illustrate how the failure of a school to take its community with it can have a dramatic impact on everyone concerned. In an Inner London school, a small group of staff introduced radical changes to the way children were taught. They introduced elements of freedom of choice and individualized learning, seeing 'the system of teaching adopted by the school as a vehicle for social change' (Auld, 1976: para 185). The school became an arena for a classic battle between 'progressive' radicals on the one hand and 'conservatives' on the other; one side advocating the child's essential goodness and readiness to learn within a class-ridden and prejudiced society; the other promoting the importance of basic skills and the need for children to conform to expectations in order to maintain the stability of society:

> The two-year power struggle at William Tyndale brought into sharp relief the question 'Who controls schools?' It created demands for a clearer settlement between local authorities, teachers, school governors and parents. It raised issues about teacher professionalism, the autonomy of headteachers, the authority of governors and the rights of parents. Events at Tyndale were as much about the fragmentation of responsibilities between the inspectorate, governors, staff, teachers and parents as a dispute over power. Tyndale also demonstrated conflicting definitions of progressive education and differing interpretations of the needs and aspirations of working-class children.
> (Riley, 1998: 50)

The William Tyndale episode was played out in the full glare of the media's attention. Both sides tried to enlist the national newspapers, while bemused parents wondered what to make of it and whom to believe. As at the Ridings schools some twenty years later, some members of the media both exploited, and were exploited by, the players:

> The teachers were subjected to daily scrutiny and personal abuse in some papers. Among the pupils at William Tyndale was Paul Harter, who later became a film editor. He recalls the school as being a 'wild' one in which the children used to 'chuck milk bottles at each other out of windows'. He also has vivid recollections of the role of the media. 'We used to go journalist baiting, tell them all the lies you could imagine. This was an added bit of fun for us. We made up some great stories. We would find out what they wanted to know and

we would make it up for them. There were always one or two
around the gate. The news and the BBC were the most exciting.
We'd be shouting obscenities'. Children such as Paul Harter
undoubtedly relished the lime-light and contributed to the
press near hysteria.

(Riley, 1998: 50)

The media campaign culminated in a bizarre game of Chinese
Whispers, whereby an exercise given by the deputy headteacher to
his class based on a quotation from William Blake – 'The tigers of
wrath are wiser than the horses of instruction' – was turned by the
Daily Mail into a line from Chairman Mao: 'The smile on the face
of the tiger is revolution.' This single event might have stood as a
metaphor for the entire episode.

By the autumn of 1976, the public had been well warmed up for a
polemical debate about the nature and purpose of schooling. One of
the major themes explored by the media over the ten years since
Risinghill was 'Are schools giving us what we want – or what we
need?' The overriding answer given by the media, on behalf of the
public, seemed to be 'probably not'. The media message was 'Give
us order and results.' Meanwhile, education professionals were
caricatured as saying, 'We will help your children to be happy and
fulfilled. If they get a few certificates too, so much the better.' Of
course, the scenario was far more complicated than that. Grace
(1972) found that there was a much higher level of agreement
between teachers and parents about the desired ends of schooling
than was being presented in a simplified way by some of Fleet
Street. Parents *were* keen that their children should be happy and
fulfilled in school – though not to the total exclusion of academic
success. Teachers wanted order and achievement, too. But the lines
were being drawn. The dramatic intervention of the Prime Minister,
Jim Callaghan, brought the debate into the political arena.

The end of consensus

Until 1976, everyone knew what they wanted from schools. Well,
not quite, perhaps. But certainly much of the media behaved as if
all that we expected of schools was self-evident. There was little or
no debate outside the profession about the content of education –
about what schools were supposed to *give* to children. In a speech

delivered at Ruskin College, Oxford, in October 1976, Callaghan questioned the direction that education seemed to have been following over the previous few years – a view apparently based on his reading of the national press! He asked what the public, and what the government, had a right to expect of the education profession. Bernard Donoughue, who wrote much of the speech, had had his own children educated in Islington – giving the inner-city London borough a claim to be the driving force for all educational change over the succeeding years. Unsurprisingly, then, Donoughue's view seemed as simplistic and as polarized as that of the media: 'education was what really mattered. All this was being ruined by a bunch of middle-class ideologues who did not themselves have a proper experience of state education.' (Interestingly, this argument has been echoed much more recently, when people arguing that early years' education should be largely exploratory rather than didactic and content-based have been accused of middle-class elitism.)

Donoughue continues:

> their prejudices were at the expense of working-class children. There was clear evidence that working-class parents and children wanted education and what they wanted was not the same as the middle-class Labour people from Islington, the trendy lecturers from higher education who wanted education at the expense of working-class kids. Jim [Callaghan] and I talked about this. Whenever I heard those people talk I got very angry. . . . Their thinking was based on *Guardian* style ideologies and prejudices.
>
> (Riley, 1998: 59)

And mine, Donoughue might have added to this balanced reasoning, is founded in *Sun*-style hysterics.

Whatever lay behind it, Callaghan's speech put education for the first time firmly at the centre of political debate.

What schools owe to the public

The major impact of Callaghan's speech, and of the twenty years of radical educational legislation that followed it – albeit enacted by another party in government – was to increase dramatically the accountability of schools to their public. The public gained access to a far wider range of information about schools – unimaginably more than they had in the 1960s. But, of course, much of this information was mediated by the media. If you really wanted to know a school's standing in the community, the local paper was still the place to look.

Much of the legislation throughout the Conservative regime of 1979–97 focused on removing or nullifying the powers of local government. The Department for Education and Employment (DfEE) (which became the Department for Education and Skills, DfES, in June 2001) took unprecedented powers over the content and structures of schooling, while the management of schools was handed over to headteachers and governing bodies. For the first time, there was a benchmark – or rather a series of benchmarks – against which schools could be judged: external examination results, test results (SATs), attendance, exclusions, even 'value for money' became elements in the comparison of one school to another on apparently objective grounds. Eventually, the intake of schools, as well as their outputs, could be judged against each other, so giving some idea of the *actual* impact that a school has on its pupils. In the wrong hands, of course, this could give further grounds for condemning 'sink' schools by intake rather than output.

The Green Paper which followed Callaghan's speech (DES, 1977) called for schools to have 'a greater awareness of the community at large; the needs of the nation as a whole; the working of a modern industrial society; and the role of an individual participating in a democracy' (DES, 1997: 37). Once again, it was possible to welcome an explicit statement of what schools were for – although many people might not agree with Callaghan's answers. The inevitable outcome of schools having a greater awareness of the community was that communities would develop a greater awareness of schools. There would be less stereotyping: parents would develop a greater sense of ownership of their children's school; schools would be seen as both serving *and* reflecting their communities. Schools would become inextricably tied into their communities and society at large instead of remaining – as many felt – divorced from the rigours of real life: of expectations of productivity, of limited budgets, and of being answerable to the people who provide their money. 'It was left to the new Conservative government, however, to enact legislation between 1980 and 1982 that brought parent and teacher representatives onto all governing bodies for the first time; made the agenda and minutes of governors' meetings available to the public; defined the governors' role in working towards a planned and coherent curriculum; and required the publication of HMI [Her Majesty's Inspectorate of Schools] reports on schools' (Gann, 1998).

These first steps in accountability did not impinge too heavily on schools. HMI reports tended to be anodyne, maintaining the tradition that the advisory function of inspection was more important than the critical function. However, the new system of inspection, introduced in 1993, fitted in with an era when measurement, league tables and 'name and shame' formed the prevailing culture.

Participation and accountability

By 1980, a substantial majority of local authorities had arrangements for parents to be represented on their school governing bodies. But the 1980 Act made this requirement in law, required all local authorities to conform to a national formula for composition, and legitimized the role of parents as governors. This meant not only that schools had become to some extent accountable to their parent body (if only a very small part of it), but that (some) parents were given an insight into school management and decision-making. With the introduction of local management of schools, this became an insight into a very significant process. Some parents had to struggle with local authorities who were reluctant to let them play a full role, despite what the law said. Others faced headteachers and other governors who claimed that they were not there to represent the parent body; or who accused them of being anecdotal, or inappropriately focused only on their own children. Schools and local authorities still, in the main, felt that there was no role for the public in knowing about, let alone in governing, schools.

A sea change was brought about in the later years of the 1980s. First, the 1986 (No. 2) Education Act (DfEE, 1986) gave further scope for involvement in (and perhaps ownership) of schools. No longer was the local authority the only – or even the majority – appointing body for school governors. Each governing body of a maintained school now comprised four 'constituencies': parents, the LEA, the staff and the local community. Governors elected by parents and teachers and those appointed from the neighbourhood of the school now found themselves with access to information previously confined to local authority officers and headteachers. This information was about both inputs and outputs – about the way finances were distributed among schools, and about the performance of schools.

However, this information was still very patchy. Some LEAs considered it good practice to delegate as much responsibility as possible to schools. Others held on to far more self-protective strategies. The breaking down of a culture in which schools were managed by local officers would take more than a simple reorganization of the membership of governing bodies. The Education Reform Act of 1988 aimed to do just that. It required LEAs to delegate the large majority of their education finances to schools – that is, to governing bodies – to spend according to *their* priorities. With the legislation simultaneously introducing the idea of entirely self-managing ('grant-maintained') schools, this was (as it was meant to be) a great blow against the powers of local government. A further undermining of the educational role of county and town halls was the introduction of the national curriculum. In this case, the powers were centralized rather than derogated.

Nevertheless, governing bodies – now predominantly lay local people – took on decision-making responsibility for the school budget, staffing, the delivery of the curriculum, much of the premises. As might be expected, the impact of this minor revolution varied enormously. The factors which affected it included:

- the willingness of LEAs to embrace the spirit of the legislation;
- the willingness of headteachers to work in partnership with predominantly lay governors;
- The presence within the community of individuals willing to work with – and to challenge – the educational establishment (a capacity, interestingly, which was not wholly dependent on the social class of the neighbourhood served by the school).

One element which was consistent nationwide was the enthusiasm of the government to ensure that the new governing bodies got involved with the *business* of the schools, without necessarily facilitating their ability to get to grips with the *principles* of the school. So, for many governors, the potential for democratization was undermined by the way the schools seemed only to want to enlist their help in furthering an agenda already set by the staff. If the governing body were to act as 'critical friend' – a phrase much favoured by government and now enshrined in statutory guidance

(DfEE, 2000) – many schools wanted only the friendship without the criticism.

Even so, as time went on throughout the 1990s, with ever more initiatives thrust on an often unwilling public (regular OfSTED inspection, literacy and numeracy hours, publication of test results, greater delegation through 'fair funding', performance management), governing bodies began to 'grow up'. Until recently, schools had had regular visits from advisers and inspectors to help the head and staff in managing; financial staff managed school budgets from county and town halls; local authorities took major responsibility for school organization and relationships with parents; PR departments managed school–media relationships; governor support departments trained governors. With the reduction in LEA resources, schools had to take on the brunt of this work. Newspapers and broadcasters no longer went to a council official for information about a school or about something that had happened in it. Now they could look up the latest inspection report on the net, visit the headteacher, phone any – or all – of the governors.

It wasn't long before the governing body came to be one of the most significant sources of information about a school's affairs. By the turn of the twenty-first century, governing bodies (at least in theory) knew as much about how well a school was doing as any professional or local politician. They might also be less cagey than heads, officers or councillors. Sometimes their frustration with bureaucratic obstructiveness or obfuscation led them into misguided revelations; sometimes they felt that the press was more likely to be on their side than not. Sometimes they took seriously the DfEE declaration that governing bodies should be accountable to their communities as well as to their LEAs. Many governors saw themselves as locked into a chain of accountability, involving the children, their parents and the local community, the LEA, the DfEE.

The headteachers

Many headteachers saw the benefits of the new accountabilities. Whereas some had enjoyed the autonomy of the role, others recognized the real benefits of a partnership with the community. Sometimes this merely took the heat off them. A secondary headteacher in the North-east was being pressed for a public statement about a teachers' walkout in her school. The cause was the reinstatement by the LEA of a pupil whose exclusion had been confirmed by the governors. The head's statement began: 'The governing body has instructed me to say. . .'. The strength given to this head's position by a (however spurious) democratic legitimacy should not be underestimated.

The schools which gained unwanted national publicity in the second half of the twentieth century were those where *either* a philosophy of education was being implemented which failed to take with it current local thinking, *or* where order had broken down. It might be argued that in either case the blame for the notoriety could be laid at the headteacher's door. Either they had failed to explain coherently to the community the beliefs and evidence underlying what they were doing, or they were unable to run a school in the way that they were trying to do. Arguably, Countesthorpe and Risinghill schools were examples of the former. Some commentators claimed that the headteachers had failed to communicate with their communities. The cases of the Ridings School in Calderdale, Hackney Downs and Phoenix schools in London, all in the 1990s, were arguably different. Each was dubbed by the press at some time 'the worst school in England'. At William Tyndale School, again arguably, the headteacher's philosophy led to a school regime which others interpreted as being a total loss of control.

By the 1990s, we might have expected to see a far greater sophistication in the way schools dealt with the press. However, most maintained schools still relied heavily on their local authority press offices if things went wrong. A detailed study of one *cause célèbre* of the decade, however, shows how a partnership between a headteacher accustomed to running his own show – coming from the grant-maintained sector – and his LEA led to a complete, and very effective, rethinking of how to handle the national (indeed, at times, international) media.

The 'school from Hell'

The public vilification of the Ridings School on the outskirts of the Yorkshire town of Halifax began in 1996. The Ridings existed due to the amalgamation of two secondary schools serving the neighbourhood. Both the amalgamation itself and its aftermath were badly mishandled by the local authority, argues the incoming headteacher, Peter Clark (Clark, 1998). The members of the LEA failed to give appropriate support to the headteacher of the new school, who was faced with two sets of parents and staff, many of whom had fought tooth and nail either to protect the status quo, or to have the new school sited where they wanted it. Staff were required to apply for their new jobs, and many lost status. Meanwhile, the members of the LEA were operating a panel for appeals against pupil exclusion which was weighted heavily in favour of the appellant parents and children. The crunch came when a girl was permanently excluded for a second time for violent behaviour and, for a second time, was reinstated by the LEA panel. This achieved national press coverage and was the first indication to the public that things were going badly awry. When Peter Clark, an experienced local headteacher, agreed to take over the school for a temporary period, he was warned by Calderdale's Assistant Director of Policy and Planning that 'This is all going to be *News at Ten* stuff, you can forget the *Halifax Evening Courier*' (ibid.: 20). This turned out to be something of an understatement.

Within a week, publicity had shifted from the *Yorkshire Evening Post* to the national media. *The Times* published an editorial on the school, BBC *Panorama* positioned cameras in the flats overlooking the school so that they could shoot scenes of disorder in a newly qualified teacher's classroom, and reporters and photographers routinely pitched camp outside the school. The presence of the press – including a team from the American network CNN – initially encouraged the very sort of behaviour they were there to report and condemn. The sense of disintegration within the school – shared by pupils, staff, governors and the LEA – led to constant leaks to the press which, presumably, were intended to further personal agendas: 'As I was to find out in future months, much confidential information about the Ridings was communicated directly to the *Yorkshire Post*. Many months later, I found out who had leaked this story, and I believe that they were trying to stop me taking up the position, or at least to make it more difficult' (ibid.: 34–5).

Clark initially tried to 'deal' with the press, arranging photoshoots and interviews in exchange for some periods of privacy, but these were 'worthless'. The media representatives, very clearly, were setting the agenda. Clark's strategy with the press, however, was similar to his strategy with the school pupils, staff and councillors. This seems to have been twofold. First, it was, as far as possible, to tell the truth about what was going on and what his intentions were. Second, it was to set out clearly the boundaries to the behaviour he was prepared to accept. He drew very clear lines, and then hit back hard when people overstepped them.

As the school was reopened after the half-term closure, Clark and his colleagues started to take over the agenda. They decided when and where to appear before the press, they negotiated offers from the BBC to pool interview and other footage, in order to avoid repetition. Following a collective photoshoot, 'The staff thought I was wonderful. I had got the press, a major disincentive to good discipline, off the street' (ibid.: 62). Later, he writes: 'my attempts to work with, rather than against, the media were resulting in a marked change in the way the school was portrayed. The coverage was much more positive: it began to concentrate on the issues and how we hoped to tackle them and less on the sensationalist "school from Hell" or Superhead angles' (ibid.: 68). When Clark refers to 'the issues', of course he means, crucially, *his* issues rather than those of the media. By this time, pupils were cooperating with Sky TV to produce an 'authorized' video diary of events. Newspapers were publishing the delighted reports of local employers taking Ridings pupils on work experience.

Further problems arose, of course, but they seem to have been isolated examples which were running against the prevailing tide. Individuals outside the 'Ridings team' which Clark had effectively created, and who had not been brought on board, were now more likely to cause problems. The secretary of a local primary school wrote to the press complaining about Ridings pupils' behaviour. A neighbour to the school said he would complain publicly if a fence were not erected to prevent pupils crossing his garden. The staff learned from this. Contractors were hurriedly brought in to do the practical job, thus removing the cause for complaint. This combination of effective press management and swift practical remedial action put the school back in charge of its future. Clark began to take the publicity initiative. A series of jokes about the school included in the Bradford pantomime that Christmas led to the star Frank Bruno being invited to the school. Publicity was being used now to change the school's image: 'One day', said Calderdale's Chief Adviser to Schools, 'they [the LEA] will understand that this has been a tremendously effective PR operation – even though it happened by accident!' (ibid.: 139). By this time, the school was able to adopt a standard response to press inquiries – 'Come round and see for yourself':

It would have been understandable if we had tried to keep the press at arm's length after the sensational and biased reporting that described the Ridings School as 'the worst school in Britain' and 'the school from Hell'. The stress of trying to work normally with the world's press lined up outside, some of them encouraging pupils to misbehave, is difficult to imagine. However, I felt it was better to manage the media interest, and build positive relationships with journalists. In the end the good news story ran longer than the negative crisis publicity and helped improve the recruitment of pupils and the morale of the whole school.

(Ibid.: 206–7)

What seems to have happened in this dramatic example of school–media relationships was that disorder could be fostered by the press in the interests of an initially 'good' story, precisely because there was no sense of collegiate responsibility in the school – neither among the pupils, nor the staff, nor much of the LEA. Clark was able to persuade the 'stakeholders' that their best interests lay in collectivity and a shared sense of belonging – feelings fostered, ironically, by the siege mentality which was the only sensible reaction to the media. Again ironically, this positive response gave the press an extended story. The public can take only so much disaster and mayhem. As Clark and his colleagues pulled the school together, a story of triumph snatched from the jaws of disaster began to emerge. From now on, just as in an effectively functioning family, visitors found that behaviour actually improved in the presence of outsiders.

The learning

Schools have come a long way in the course of little more than ten years. Much of the story is of success – of ever-improving standards at all ages, of a growing consensus about the purpose of schooling. But there are significant battles still to be won. Behaviour and order in schools – especially among boys – is as much of an issue as ever. Standards in the basics are still thought by many to be too low. The principal divide – between those who believe that children (and schools) flourish better by support and encouragement than they do by challenge and denigration – still exists. It is now very much part of the public domain. It is therefore, rightly, of consuming interest to the media.

Simultaneously, the very media are expanding beyond all recognition. The newspapers get ever thicker and need more and more to fill them. Television viewers not only have an unimaginably wider choice of channels, but will soon have complete control over what to watch and when to watch it.

The new worlds of education and the media offer us an exciting and a worrying challenge. In the remainder of this book, we hope to offer some routes through the labyrinth that awaits us.

Chapter 2

Schools and the media
Getting the relationship right

Dispelling some myths about the media.
Why schools need to make contact with
newspapers and broadcasting organizations.

Media people: some stereotypes

The public relations (PR) industry is going through something of an image crisis right now. We need only think of the stories in the newspapers of the manipulative 'spin doctors' from the political world and the well-heeled, well-lubricated and larger-than-life characters in the comedy series *Absolutely Fabulous* to see why that is the case. School governing bodies surely don't want to get mixed up with that lot! Anyway, we've got more than enough to do looking after the finances, staffing and the leaking roof without having to deal with the murky world of the media. What's more, we're up to our pupil numbers' limit already and we don't want any more children turning up because of an article in the paper, do we? Let's just get on with things and keep quiet.

To think like that is certainly understandable given the already wide range of tasks faced by teachers and governing bodies and our own inability to cram any more jobs into a day. But we ought at least to reflect on whether we are making the most of our school's achievements. If we have done good things, then we should let people know about it, not just staff and parents. If we have a view about a wider issue that we believe needs airing, we ought to speak out. If things go wrong, we should let people know the score from our point of view. We can only do this properly if we take a realistic look at how we communicate with the world beyond the school fence.

Why should we talk to the media?

This will certainly be an issue for school governing bodies such as those mentioned in the first paragraph, and for others who may not have thought about the question of publicity. Banner headlines in national papers rarely make good reading. They usually tell sorry tales of failure, argument or scandal. But by far the majority of stories that appear about schools in the newspapers are in the local, not the national, press. Contrary to the belief of many governors, the local media *will* print or broadcast good stories about events and achievements just as they want to report items when things have gone wrong. Of course, local media organizations are in business to make money and certainly they can do this by dramatic headlines, but their role is also to reflect local life, report events and create discussion. If we do not let the local papers and other news organizations know about the school play, the new garden, outstanding achievements by pupils or fund-raising activities for charity, then they are not going to chase us for this information. We will have missed an important opportunity to sing our own praises. Many local newspapers have supplements devoted to what is going on in schools in the area and are actively looking for good news stories about schools, especially the unusual and the offbeat. The more leads we give to the newsdesk and the more satisfactory the relationship with the journalist, the better.

There is no point in complaining that another school is in the news *again* when we have not told the paper about what we have done. That other school is likely to have taken the initiative. This is *proactive* PR, which *we* initiate. We identify an achievement and package it nicely for journalists and give them what they want. In some ways, we have to think like a journalist and submit newsworthy items and not bombard the newsdesk with trivia or inappropriate messages. More than 90 per cent of news releases from all sources end up in the editor's bin. Given the need to make the best use of our time, we must make sure that there is a good chance of our contribution making it into the successful 10 per cent. However, ultimately it is up to the journalist to choose whether to write the story or to throw it away.

When things go wrong in a school and headteachers or chairs of governing bodies are asked to comment, it is usually advisable to talk to the media and return their calls. The published alternatives of 'refused to comment' or 'the headteacher was unavailable' carry their own message to readers. In general terms, for effective communication in a crisis, the school should speak with one voice, and so only the headteacher, the chair of governors or a designated deputy should deal with the media.

An associated area is crisis management, which is a much misunderstood term. While some schools may regard this as lurching from one crisis to another, as many of us will have experienced in our own working lives, this is not the appropriate definition. Crisis management relates to a prepared plan of action which can be implemented when something goes wrong. Most schools implement a media crisis-management plan in winter with possible school closures through bad weather. Although it is not appropriate to go to the extreme lengths taken by some industries in drawing up contingency plans, it is useful to devise a general policy of managing communication with the media when we are faced with bad news or adverse publicity. This is public relations on a reactive basis, when we are approached by the media organizations.

Another area where we react to events is when the headteacher is approached by local media to comment on a national or local issue connected with education, for example, the end of key-stage tests, stress within the profession, the disparity in funding between various local authority areas and so on. Following up national stories is a standard activity carried out by local journalists, but the initiative can also be taken by the school through the head or chair contacting newspapers and other media directly to put their points. You take the initiative and get into print or on the air. Journalists like to know of people who are prepared to talk knowledgeably and authoritatively about educational topics, and they will note in their 'contact book' whether the individual comes across well in their medium. If he or she does, then they can count on more phone calls for comment in the future. In general, the more publicity you get, both positive and general comment, the better.

Are the media out to get you?

Getting positive publicity for your school is always a good thing. Parents, staff, children and governors will all be proud of the achievements and the recognition which come from a good 'write-up', photo or broadcast. But all too often when a journalist phones to follow up a story, heads become nervous and go on the defensive. Is it too much trouble to sort things out for the journalist? Will they write the wrong thing? What can we do to make the most of this opportunity? How can we make this different and dynamic? How can we help it to stand out from the other education stories in the paper?

Do your homework!

There is little point in getting riled with children who don't do their homework if we don't do it ourselves. It may well be our job to help the journalist, particularly if they are piecing together a positive story about us. But above all, it is crucial to make sure the image of the school, or issue we are being asked to comment on, is conveyed accurately both to the journalist and subsequently to readers, viewers or listeners. We need to make sure we have considered all the areas the journalist is likely to ask questions about and come up with an appropriate response. We will look at this in more detail in Chapter 3. If it looks as if there's going to be a negative story about us, the same rules apply. We need to have a firm grasp of the situation and know our answers to likely questions. Techniques to get on top of this situation are discussed in Chapter 4.

Believe it or not, journalists usually display some human characteristics

The purpose of an interview is to explore a particular topic of the journalist's choosing, to obtain more information, and often to consider how it relates to other people's views. In the main, journalists deal with people fairly but people are sometimes unhappy with the way their side has been portrayed. Certainly, it is the journalist's job to get 'news', and there are days when some stories will be followed up and others when they are not. If individuals have been closely involved in an issue, it is sometimes very difficult for them to see or appreciate another person's point of view. If this alternative view is put forward in the media then this can be perceived as bias, or as the newspaper 'taking sides'. Of course, the newspaper may choose to comment on a particular issue in its editorial column: that is the prerogative of the editor. But since one of the aims of public relations is to bring about a change in perception in individuals, perhaps more effort should be made to persuade the editor, in a constructive fashion, that their position on a particular matter is flawed.

A question of perception

Sometimes a school will feel that a reporter has not put over its feelings accurately or has covered only part of an issue. This is often to do with the complexity of a story. A reporter will have a limited number of words in which to write a story. In that article the journalist will need to outline the issue and, possibly, obtain views from a number of different sources – a headteacher, local politicians, local people and so on. This means that a complicated issue often has to be condensed into a few sentences that sum up the essence of the problem. It is impossible – and undesirable for a general audience – to include all the nuances of a particular issue. A few key points will usually be covered in the article and a range of opinions, usually some for and some against. Because a journalist from a specialist publication – the *Times Educational Supplement*, for example – is not writing for a general audience, explanations and detail which would be required in the daily press are not needed. Naturally, more specialist topics are also covered in these publications.

Don't forget that the media will usually want to give coverage to the more unusual stories; for example, the return to school of a famous former pupil, or perhaps a photogenic object which a pupil has invented. Members of staff who are leaving, as well as prize-giving, may merit a few lines and a picture. This type of coverage is worthwhile – but reflect on the message you want to leave in the minds of the readers. What will be glossed over in reading, listening or viewing and what will remain in the individual's mind?

Upset at how you've been treated?

If you feel genuinely aggrieved, then speak to the editor and put your points across politely but firmly. If there is a valid cause for complaint, the editor will want to put this right as soon as possible. With local media in particular, a long-term perspective should be taken by both the school and the news organization. You need to get on with the papers and broadcasting organizations to make sure they give you good coverage next time!

A right to publicity – is there one?

In essence, the answer is 'no'. Unlike some countries where this concept is enshrined in law, there is no such statute in the UK. However, broadcasting organizations in particular are closely regulated, and have a duty to ensure that various sides of an issue or dispute are covered. This does not necessarily mean coverage within the same report or even bulletin or programme, but the opposing sides to a story should be broadcast within a realistic timescale. Newspapers do not have such close regulation, but most publications will want to get a range of opinions and comment into an article, in order to show balance. The competing views do not have to take the same prominence or be of the same length. Indeed, national newpapers often have their own agenda, which in turn will have been determined by the make-up of the readership.

Occasionally, individuals will approach newsdesks demanding coverage of a particular issue. Such an approach is unlikely to endear them to the journalist on duty or to the editor. The journalist will, usually dispassionately, review the details and decide whether to pursue the story. Similarly, when a headteacher angrily tells a journalist that 'this is not a story', then inherent curiosity will usually mean that the issue will be investigated further and the school, in all probability, will receive less than favourable coverage.

National and local media

It is often for the wrong reasons that schools appear in the national media. Unless it is a general report about an issue such as proposed government legislation accompanied by shots of children in class or A level/GSCE results day with children celebrating their success, then schools will often receive national coverage for specific difficulties they are facing.

However, the local media will tend to cover the good side of things as well as the bad. Local newspapers are community newspapers. They keep people in touch with what is happening around the corner. In all probability, schools will only have dealings with these organizations. Think about the stories you have read about schools in the national newspapers. They may be about a crisis. In the context of all the schools in the UK, coverage of these schools is very small but intense. Or they may be a comment item, usually on government policy, examination results or surveys.

Different media will have different audiences, staffing and objectives. The *Times Educational Supplement* is staffed by educational specialists. National dailies will have an education correspondent with other people supporting that individual. The local newspaper will possibly have an education correspondent, especially if the paper has a weekly education supplement. Commercial radio stations will almost certainly not have educational specialists unless that role is part of a wider remit. However, in the BBC, if there is a joint radio/television or bimedia newsroom, there will almost always be an education correspondent who will cover such matters for both radio and television. The fact that organizations do not employ specialist educational reporting staff does not mean that your story will not receive coverage. News releases will be considered by the general reporting staff, who may choose to follow up the story. Free newspapers usually have a small staff and in these publications news releases can sometimes be seen reproduced almost verbatim.

It is important to identify all the local media to make sure that contact is made with all possible relevant outlets.

Management of perception: should teachers become spin doctors?

Some people may believe that it is not the role of a school to court publicity, but that it is the job of teachers to teach children and of heads to manage the school. But, as we have seen at the Ridings School, part of the managerial role is to create and develop, for those outside, a positive local perception of the school, its staff and pupils. This can only be done by communication. The following chapters spell out why this important process is recognized and acted upon by successful schools. What we are trying to do is tell people the good things about our school. This is just common sense. Public relations is not mystical and, at a basic level, it is not difficult to achieve.

Chapter 3

Public relations

Describes some of the basic ideas used by
PR practitioners and how they are relevant
to schools. Identifying various publics and the
creation of appropriate messages.

A school is a living, vibrant entity. For almost everyone in the developed world, school has at some stage been the centre of our lives. Each school has its own personality stamped on it, not just by one individual but by the hundreds of people who make it up – teaching and non-teaching staff, children, parents and governors. Despite the best efforts of governments past and present and of OfSTED inspectors to require us to measure up to their expectations, and to conform to a common set of criteria, every educational establishment has its own character and its own identity.

In businesses, a corporate identity is developed and created by teams of consultants, sometimes with a multi-million pound budget. Its purpose is to make the organization stand out from the competition, often with a distinctive visual identity, and to attract people to purchase products or services from that brand. Of course, 'big business' sometimes gets it wrong and has to rethink the overall strategy. One case in recent years has been British Airways, which redesigned its tailfin decorations, only to find this made things more confusing for passengers and pilots. Even more significantly, it incurred the wrath of the former Prime Minister, Mrs Thatcher, who was angry that the traditional union flag design had been ditched. These firms may be able to standardize letterheads, compliments slips and uniforms, but it is the *attitude, service* and *behaviour* of an organization's staff that make or break a business. Most big firms boast a corporate communications department in order to make sure that people who work for the company know what's happening within the organization and that the customers – current and potential – get to hear about the things they want to know. Different customers have different wants and needs. The trick is to make sure that the right people get to know the right information. This can be done through advertising, but public relations (PR) plays a major part in communicating what the company is all about and what it has to offer.

No one would expect a major business to operate efficiently and effectively without properly communicating its *raison d'être* to its employees and to the wider public. Why should we expect schools to do anything different? The budgets of schools range from tens of thousands to millions of pounds, so the larger schools will have finances on a par with – perhaps greater than – many major businesses in its area. So it makes sense for headteachers and governors to put some resources into this area. People may argue that schools are not businesses and so should not be treated as such. While it is true that schools which deal with developing young people academically, culturally, socially and physically have a different overall goal from that of businesses, the ethos of efficiency and value for money within the school is both a sensible and necessary element. Both schools and businesses have financial constraints within which they have to work, and targets which have to be met. The difference is that the business will be given a percentage profit target while the school will usually have a target of breakeven or maintenance of a small surplus.

This chapter introduces some of the key concepts of PR. These are the same whether you are a small primary school or a multi-national organization.

What is public relations?

A typical response from undergraduates studying for a communication or business degree would be that public relations is 'free advertising'. It would be useful if this comment were to come at the beginning of the course, when the student would soon be rid of this notion. PR is not free, neither is it advertising. With advertising, an organization agrees a price to publish a specific message at a particular time and in a specific place in a newspaper ot magazine, or with a broadcasting company. The organization knows what is contained in the advertisement and has total control over where and when it appears. With PR, there is very little control. You are reliant on your ability to write a newsworthy item in a persuasive manner so that the editor or journalist decides to include it in the publication or broadcast. Of course, because you have no control over what is published, the media might take a view on the matter which is different from yours and use that as a basis for another type of story – one which is not what you intended at all. For example, if a sports centre produces a release which states somewhere that 75 per cent of people using the swimming pools are happy with the lifeguards and swimming supervision, the media are likely to turn this around and say that 25 per cent of people are not, and ask you for comment! It is always worthwhile thinking how other people could interpret the way you put your message across.

PR is described by the Institute of Public Relations (IPR) as 'the planned and sustained effort to establish and maintain goodwill between an organization and its publics'.

For many of us, it is the spin doctors who have come to the fore in politics in recent years who have given public relations a bad name. But no more so than the untrained PR people who present themselves as experts. Practitioners do not have to be members of any professional organization; companies putting themselves forward as PR agencies do not have to have had any experience or success in this field before setting up. The simple fact is that a significant number of firms claiming to offer PR services do not know what PR is or understand its functioning. They charge exorbitant fees for limited service: some are no better than cowboy builders who charge an arm and a leg for badly nailing on a few roof tiles. Just as reputable builders are sometimes tarred with the same brush as the cowboys, good PR businesses have to put up with the fear and scepticism of potential clients who don't know what they want and don't know what they're getting. Whereas the cowboy builder usually makes the pages of the local newspaper, the poorly run PR agency does not. Following the analogy, this chapter concentrates on how to do basic, do-it-yourself PR.

PR is 'a planned and sustained effort'. PR is not just a 'one off' or something which happens. Much thought and attention need to be given to the messages you wish to send out to people and how this is going to be achieved. What events are taking place, what initiatives are under way that can be taken forward into print or onto the air-waves? The recruitment and retention of pupils is a key area for all schools. How do parents whose children are not yet at your school get an impression of how your school fares in comparison to other establishments? How does your school deal with drugs education or bullying?

The overall purpose of PR, and publicity in general, will reflect one or more of three basic aims:

1   to put information in someone's mind;
2   to try to change or shape someone's mind;
3   to get someone to do something.

To some, this may seem scheming and unethical but it is no more than putting your own views forward and getting them heard. Indeed, the easiest way to get bad publicity is to lie or cover up a particular issue.

PR is *planned*, in that you have to identify what you want to achieve. Who do you want to talk to? What message do you want to get over? Will it get in the media at all? PR must also be *sustained*; that is, it must be delivered creatively, but conform to some systematic guidelines. One positive item appearing in a local newspaper may be seen as a success, but that image will stay in people's minds only fleetingly. The positive message needs to be continually reinforced to make sure it stays in people's minds.

Another element in the definition of 'public relations' is the *maintenance of goodwill* – in other words, for people to be positive (or at least not negative) about what you do. If schools can manage their image and reputation effectively, then much groundwork will have been done to help establish and develop links between the school and the wider community.

Publics

This book certainly does not concentrate on jargon, but one term needs to be explained as it is one of the keys to successful PR activity. That word is, in the IPR definition, 'publics'. It can be described as 'all those groups of people with which [the organization] is or wants to be in communication' (Harrison, 1995). Other people choose the term 'stakeholders', which has been favoured by government spokespersons in recent years. One definition is 'those individuals or groups who depend on the organization to fulfil their own goals and on whom, in turn, the organisation depends' (Johnson and Scholes, 1999). For an ordinary business it would include employees, customers, suppliers, shareholders. In PR for schools, typical 'publics' can be seen as pupils, staff, LEA, parents (both actual and potential), local residents, local businesses and councillors. This concept of 'publics' can be divided further into 'internal publics' and 'external publics'. Schools need to keep people within the organization – staff and pupils – well informed as well as those outside the organization. A business would not normally class customers as an 'internal public' as they are usually readily free to take their custom elsewhere. But because pupils have such a close and long-term relationship with the school, it could be argued that they too should be regarded as 'internal publics'. This could also be argued because the pupils' input and contribution affect how the school will be judged.

Let us look at some of the 'external publics' and consider why we might need to get particular messages across to them:

- *Parents of pupils at the school*: the need to keep them informed so they know what their children are being taught, are aware of current issues within the school, of development of the school, and of planned and possible changes – consultation.
- *Parents of children below admission age for a particular school*: to present the ethos and values of your school accurately so that parents can make an informed decision on admission application.
- *The local education authority (and, for church schools, the diocese)*: to give public evidence of how funds are managed – e.g. implementation of school initiatives – to raise issues of special relevance to the school, to give a public response to a particular local matter – such as parents' parking – and generally to show a responsible and proactive attitude to the school's role in the broader community; possibly also to raise public awareness of an issue so the LEA or diocese has to take notice.
- *Councillors*: they still hold some of the purse-strings locally, make decisions on the future of schools through funding, capital projects and so on. Councillors are representatives of the wider community we serve. They need to know what the issues are and we need to make sure they know if there are specific issues which affect us.
- *Members of Parliament*: responsible for the raft of central government initiatives (or opposition to them). We need to ensure that the reality of implementation is reflected in our messages to them. Also in their remit are particular regulatory issues which affect us and which we may wish to see changed – e.g. funding boundaries.
- *Local employers*: for secondary schools, a source of jobs for pupils, work experience, sponsorship and know-how; development and management of partnerships are likely to be valuable.

For primary schools, visits, talks and sponsorship are worthwhile, probably on a smaller scale. Potential governors may be found among them. Also represented are the local Chamber of Commerce and Industry and organizations such as Rotary and Round Table. They need to be made aware of the school's contribution to the community through pupils' and teachers' activity and achievement, as well as to know that their own contribution is valued.

- *Community groups*: getting information across to people we perhaps wouldn't otherwise reach, bringing people in from these groups to give pupils a glimpse of a culture which is different from theirs, including disability awareness and other associated issues of equal opportunities.
- *Former pupils*: they contribute to society in many ways. They link our pupils with the world after school. For primary schools, former pupils can help in the transition from infant to junior or primary to secondary. It makes for a smoother changeover all round!
- *Local residents*: giving people without children at the school an insight into the work of the school and the academic and extra-curricular achievements of pupils and staff. This may help to offset residents' frustration at noise and parental car-parking – or it may not! Schools must try to be good neighbours without being walked over. A responsible, mature and open attitude, together with a desire to share the good news of the school with people who live nearby, should be encouraged.
- *OfSTED*: press cuttings and other media appearances can serve to boost the profile of a school at inspection time. While other criteria at this time take centre stage, a judicious selection of articles can assist in developing the inspection team's perception in a positive manner and supporting or bolstering the findings of the inspectors' consultation with parents.
- *The local media*: a public in their own right. Many local newspapers have a regular education supplement featuring news and comment about schools, together with articles and contributions from pupils. The newspapers need a supply of appropriate comment and sources for interview. While inclusion of articles in the local press is not guaranteed, the development of a good working relationship with journalists will pay off. Radio and television stations also have news magazine programmes. The media are the means by which you can reach other people.

What is news?

What is going to get your school in the news? A definition that is a continual source of debate in newsrooms and on journalism courses is 'what exactly is news?' There is no one accepted definition. But news has to do with things that people want to know. It is about *people*.

In a financial story, the effect of a drop in profits for a company will result in redundancies and restructuring – the effect on people. In a school, a new building will mean better conditions for pupils and teaching and support staff in two years' time, but it will cause problems while building work is going on at the site. It may mean difficulties for some parents in getting children to school. Local people may have to put up with more congestion. Will the building go ahead as planned in spite of the council's aim to keep the council tax down? Although the building is needed because of an increase in the number of children in that area, the project may be delayed for several years in order not to create a bigger bill for people who pay council tax. You will see that the issue which made this news is not the building itself but the *effect* the planned building will or may have on different people – or publics.

Journalists will usually look for the 'people' angle. Although they are trained to hunt out this aspect, if it is highlighted for them in the title and first few lines of the release they will take your message more seriously. This is considered in greater detail in Chapter 4. In OfSTED reports, for example, comments about a well-managed school can be translated into news by stressing that staff in the school provide the best education for the children. This switches the emphasis from management of resources to the effect on children. This does not mean you cannot talk about the praise a school has received from the OfSTED inspectors in providing value for money and managing curriculum and financial issues, but that you need to bring to the fore (certainly at the outset) what this means for the people in the publics you are targeting. The 'people' angle will grab the journalist's attention and interest, who will now set about either writing a story on what has been contained in a news release (and summary OfSTED report) or telephone you for more information and a chance to get some opinions on the report.

What is news will also differ from person to person and from publication to publication. In writing a news release, you should think back to the publics you are trying to talk to. What are you trying to tell them? Who are the people who read the newspaper or listen to the radio, and what do they want to know? The vast majority of news releases which are received by news organizations are thrown away after a cursory read by the editor or journalist on duty. This is because the content quite clearly does not conform to the 'news needs' of that organization. It is a standard part of the day's work for the journalist to go through the post sent to the newsdesk. As many as 100 press releases may hit the desk on any particular day. How many will move to the next stage of consideration? The typical result would be four or five definite stories and a similar number of 'possibles'. The rest will end up in the bin straight away.

What is news for a school, in addition to the 'people' angle, is something that is unusual. For example:

- *The first time something has happened* – pupils with A-starred grades at A level or the oldest or youngest pupil to achieve a particular grade. Stories to do with examination results need to be communicated to media organizations immediately the results are released: newspapers will not want to cover stories about A levels two or three days after the result date – this will be dead news by then. Use the fax and telephone!
- *The last time something will happen* – e.g. the retirement of a long-serving teacher or the last day before a school moves to another building – the school might focus on what was happening in the world when the school first opened in the nineteenth century, and on what has happened since. Have there been any famous pupils? Has anyone famous visited the school? Who is the longest-serving member of staff or the oldest ex-pupil? Have any dramatic incidents happened at the school? How did staff cope with the children in the Second World War? In some ways, the school which is being closed down has become personified and has experienced a life itself. You are telling the life of the building. It will appeal to the many thousands of pupils who have passed through the school. Of course, this could become a major project and eat up a signifi-cant amount of time. How about setting a school project so the children can research the issues? The key findings can be written up and people made available for interview or comment. A basic news release could be drawn up, but a potentially detailed topic such as this could be the basis for a feature in

the local newspaper or radio station. In this case, this would need to be discussed in advance with the media organizations so that you would be guaranteed some coverage and both the school and media organization would know what is expected of each other.

- *Comment on a national issue affecting your school actually or potentially* – e.g. the difference in school funding between the home counties and the rest of the UK ; the anomaly over fees for English students going to Scottish universities; performance 'league tables'. These would be issues which affect people and about which headteachers would have a view. Views which meekly agree with policies or actions taken are less likely to get into print or on air. If they do, they are unlikely to receive as much prominence as those which criticize. The media like to create debate, or argument, about issues. The readers and listeners like to read and hear about controversy.

Journalists will treat news in a variety of ways. You will need to identify the sort of news your school either wants to put across or is faced with. You must then decide how best to present it. The categories are essentially to do with whether the news from your point of view is bad or good and the length of any likely article.

Hard news v. soft news

Hard news stories in schools are usually the ones you would rather not see published. They may tell of the misdemeanours of a member of staff, major incidents of vandalism, fire at the school or accidents involving pupils or staff. How best to handle these issues is discussed in Chapter 5. We will be approached by the media for comment in these cases, so we have to have a strategy to deal effectively with the issues.

Soft news stories are those which are of interest to people but not of dramatic importance. Soft news stories are likely to make up much of the material we send to newspapers, magazines and broadcasting organizations.

News v. features

This distinction has relevance mainly to the probable length of the piece. News is short, punchy and to the point. A news item on local radio may be 15 seconds long if it is read by the news presenter, or a probable maximum of 40 seconds if it contains a recorded comment from a person involved with the story. In radio news bulletins, the individual length of items is unlikely to be longer than this. The television station may run a slightly longer piece in a bulletin. The newspaper may give two or three columns to a current news story. There is, however, another part of newspaper content or radio/ television output which allows a greater development of material: the feature. This is a longer item which will involve interviews, and the search for more information and photographs or filming (for the print and television media). Television journalists will build a feature for use in their evening news magazine programmes and take out part of the final item for use in the news bulletin later that evening. Large commercial radio stations have reduced their feature output significantly in recent years, but the newer, smaller community stations rely on local input so this is a growing potential media outlet. BBC local radio stations are typically speech based and so have more scope for features. Local and national newspapers often have education supplements and this is where features to do with schools are usually to be found.

If you have a good relationship with the local media you can 'sound them out' to find out if they would be likely to run a feature on an aspect of the school. If this is an aspect of 'soft news', as it typically would be, then you would need to think in advance of ways to persuade the journalist to consider your request favourably. You must focus on the 'people' aspect of the feature which the journalist will be looking for.

Action points

1   Identify the publics for your school. Extend the list given in this chapter. Why are the publics important to you and what do they want to know?
2   Examine the media coverage your school has received in the past two years.
    (a) Which media have given you coverage?
    (b) What sort of coverage – positive/negative, hard/soft, news/ features?
    (c) What have you done to get positive media comment in this period?

3   Think of at least four items over the past year which could have brought you media coverage and how you might have made these items attractive to a journalist.

Chapter 4

News releases

Getting the message across

Describes how a news release can be compiled
to get your message out to the media.
Why you are doing this. Some dos and don'ts.

The news release

What it is

A news release is the basic way by which you get in touch with the
people who are able to put your message across. Most textbooks and
even public relations (PR) practitioners will call this a 'press release'.
However, it is better to use the term 'news release' because the word
'press' refers solely to newspapers, magazines and printed material.
Because of the growth in broadcast news outlets and on-line news
agencies in the UK in recent years, this title may play a part in per-
suading them whether or not to run a news story. If you use the
term 'news release', you are likely to generate a more positive feeling
within the radio journalist towards what you have to say and send a
positive first impression to the newspaper journalists as well. The old
adage that 'you don't get a second chance to make a first impression'
is true in this case. What you are sending to the news organization is
news. If it isn't, you shouldn't be sending it. At the very least, you
need to think up a more unusual way of presenting what you are
trying to say so that it becomes newsworthy.

The news release is on a piece of A4 paper, often not more than
one page and single-sided, which contains the information a journalist needs in order to understand what you are trying to say, what the
story is about and how to get more information. It is clear, concise
and well laid out, with a quote from a relevant person and contact
numbers (home/mobile as well as work/school) for a senior person
who can give more information or an interview. In fact, the release
should contain everything that a journalist would need to write in a
short piece, together with an invitation to get more detailed information and how to get it.

As we have said above, the vast majority of news releases are thrown away by journalists after nothing more than a cursory inspection. A busy newsdesk will receive hundreds of news releases each day, while a small local paper will receive several dozen. The journalists on duty will want to prioritize their time and reject any releases which do not fit into their requirements. For a local or regional media organization this usually means local news which is current and is a good story. So you have to make your release stand out from the 90 per cent or so that are thrown in the bin. The meaning of news has been discussed elsewhere but really the first question you have to ask yourself in preparing a release is why the editor of the newspaper, or radio/television station should give space and time to your story. Does what you are saying have implications for children or parents? If so, how many? Is it new information? Is it controversial? Is it humorous? Is it information which is current?

What it is not

The news release is not notification of a jumble sale. It is not a mass of facts and figures. It is not more than two pages long. It is not news about something which happened a month ago, and it is not something which has the key facts you want to say stuck in the middle of the release or right at the end as a conclusion. It is not something which has a right to be published.

How about some general tips?

Before we get into how to put a news release together, it will be helpful to look at things more closely from the journalist's point of view. Certainly, journalists are trained to seek out particular angles within a possible story, and there will be certain criteria which need to be met. Is there a specific issue which the news organization or journalist is particularly interested in? Does the news organization want or need pictures (stills, black and white or colour, audio for radio or movement for television)? We need to tempt the journalist with something which is worth publishing.

Here, we can roll out some theory, the grandly titled 'response hierarchy theory' upon which many advertisements are based. Granted, you are not advertising your school, but public relations and advertising (together with some other elements) come under the global banner of marketing communications and they rely on the same overall aim to communicate a message effectively and efficiently to a specific and defined audience: publics in PR terms.

The theory not only helps us write our news release but also forces us to think about how we, as a school, can develop a longer-term media/PR policy. PR may be a relatively new concept but the basic response hierarchy theory dates back to the 1920s in America. This model was published in Strong's *The Psychology of Selling* in 1925. In terms of PR for schools, it works because it helps us 'sell' the idea of what we want to say to the journalists we target. It relies on the principle that if the journalist is going to write a story about us, then they need to learn about the issues involved, to become so interested in what we have to say that this generates a desire to learn more about the story, which ultimately leads to action on the part of the journalist; in other words, the journalist generates a story or contacts us for further details. This is known as the AIDA model:

Attention
Interest
Desire
Action

A number of other models have developed as spin-offs from this, but the basic concept remains the same; that is to say, moving from initial awareness of an issue, idea or product/service to action. Action is doing something positive with the information, such as publishing something or, in advertising terms, buying the product or service.

How you can incorporate this goal into your news release is explained below, but the AIDA concept is useful for longer-term objectives. Promotion or PR should not be seen just as a string of news releases which are sent to all and sundry about any manner of school activities. The key is to think through an overall strategy of what you are trying to achieve with your promotional ideas. More on this later.

How do I write a good news release?

It doesn't matter how good your story is if it gets rejected at the first hurdle. If the release is well written then it will not only stand a chance of appearing in print or on the air, but some of what you have written may also appear verbatim; the news organization may also want to talk to someone connected with the story. This will often mean the headteacher, a classroom teacher or a member of the support staff, the people who are involved in the day-to-day management of the school. Remember, the journalist is not out to publish everything that is sent to the newsdesk. The acid test is to think of a good reason why a media organization *should* publish or rewrite the information you send in.

Below are some general guidelines which you can use to make the most of your story.

Make your news release look professional

Use good-quality white or light-coloured paper with the school logo and details. Make sure it is clearly headed 'News release' in bold, large capitals. You do not need special 'news release' paper; your school headed A4 paper will do. Whatever story you are sending to the media is 'news', so do not hesitate to use this term. Address it by name to the editor or educational correspondent of the media organization. The letter will usually be opened and read as normal mail to the newsdesk if addressed to the editor. There is no need to include a covering letter. Don't forget to date the release.

Use double spacing with margins on both left and right, and only use one side of the A4 paper. You might need to think about the quality of the headed paper you use. Expensive, watermarked paper may give the wrong impression. It might, however, suggest that the school cares about the information it sends out and promotes an identity of professionalism. A poorly designed news release on cheap paper is likely to create a bad impression and is simply likely to lead to the journalists developing a negative perception of your school and of the content of the release. It could also get the school a reputation within the newsroom for producing poor-quality material. Such a reputation can be difficult to shake off and may lead to good stories failing to be picked up by the newsdesk. Needless to say, the release should be word processed.

Make sure what you are saying is not 'old' news

You need to date the news release. You can post-date the release for the date of receipt by the newsdesk. It is best to use first-class post –

try to post early in the day in order to guarantee receipt the next day. Generally speaking, you should mark it 'for immediate release'. The journalist needs to know that what has been sent is current and that their organization has at least been sent the news at the same time as everybody else. Some organizations choose to head their releases with an embargo. This means that news organizations are asked not to print or publish the story or anything to do with it until a particular date and time. In practice, an embargo cannot be enforced and will usually turn a journalist away from a story. There may be pressing reasons for an organization to request that a story be held until a particular time, in which case it is useful to explain these briefly in a note at the end of the release. You must be in no doubt that journalists will be irritated by releases which try to tell them what they can and cannot do! If you are trumpeting examination successes, these need to be sent off, preferably by fax or email, on the day the results are released. These provide instant hard copy for the newsdesk. You can always check a little later by telephone to make sure that the release has been received.

Do not use the fax for general news releases, as the need for immediate transmission to the newsdesk is not apparent. It will tie up the fax machine at the news organization's office, as well as yours. With the increasing use of electronic communications, it is useful to check the news organization's policy on email. It would, of course, be self-defeating if you emailed your release to an individual journalist who was on holiday and only opened your news message on their return!

What is the story all about?

You need a good headline or title to your news release, which is short and catchy. For example, if you are referring to an OfSTED report, it might be 'Top marks for Midshire School'. The headline/title will be in bold type, a slightly larger type size than the rest of the text, and centred on the page. You can also write the title in capitals. It is a good idea to work in the title of the town or village where the school is. It reinforces the local angle for the journalist. Make sure the town you are mentioning is in the editorial area of the news organization, otherwise this is the easiest way to have your release binned! Remember to keep the title short. We recommend a maximum of about ten words. Do not use underlinings.

Be clear about who you are writing for

Most people will recognize the difference in writing styles between quality dailies such as *The Times* and the *Independent* and tabloids like the *Sun* and the *Daily Mail*. It is helpful to couch your release in the style of the publication. However, there are general rules in writing news releases which will always serve you well. This usually means writing short, simple, punchy sentences. Avoid long sentences with lots of clauses. When you proofread your release, take out some of the commas and put in full stops!

Remember, you want to get across your information as clearly and succinctly as possible. This also means cutting down on complicated language and jargon. If you use initials or an acronym, make sure you explain the meaning. Convention suggests that you write numbers up to and including ten in words, but show numbers from 11 onwards as numerals. Remember to check grammar, punctuation and syntax (especially important if the release is from a school!). A general rule is to keep things simple. The journalist only needs the key points to understand your story. They will take things on from there.

Starting off

The first sentence of the release needs to summarize the key issue. It needs to relate to one specific aspect. You might choose positive comments about new science provision, for example, or an OfSTED report might have picked out pastoral care and management of the school as the school's good points. It would be wrong to include all these points in a first sentence. In trying to keep things simple, it is tempting to cram everything positive into the first sentence. If this is too long, complicated or irrelevant, the release is likely to be rejected. The first sentence is there to arouse interest. It sets the scene for what comes later. You are trying to sort out a number of good points you want to put forward. In short, effective communication means getting your message across and moving the journalist along the Attention, Interest, Desire, Action line. Keep things simple and you will get the journalist interested.

Developing the release with more information

Develop this first line with some key points in the first paragraph.

You could now draw on some of the positive comments in the main OfSTED report or summary, which justifies your first sentence. The first sentence plainly states what you want to say. The rest of the release backs this up and adds new information. In fact, the old teaching adage may come in handy: 'One: Tell 'em what you're going to tell 'em. Two: Tell 'em. Three: Tell 'em what you've told 'em.'

What do people say?

Include some quotes from people relevant to the story. Keep the language simple and do not use education jargon. The people reading the release will be writing for the general public (unless you are targeting a specialist paper/journal). You should use people's names liberally and give the person's title. News is about people. News organizations need to know who someone is – first name and surname, not initials. This is a golden rule!

Contact details

Make sure you put at least one contact name and telephone number at the bottom of the release. At least one of the names must be able to be contacted at all times; you will need work/school and home/ mobile telephone numbers. You should make sure the names are of individuals authorized to speak on behalf of the school on the matter, that they are available to talk to the media, and that they have a prepared statement or set of comments. It is not appropriate to tell the journalist that the person concerned is 'at a meeting' unless they can be passed swiftly on to someone else. News organizations may contact you at any time once the release has been sent. People who respond to journalists by saying that they won't talk to them on a Sunday will find their release rejected. Sometimes they end up on an unofficial blacklist. It has happened! In PR terms, the news organizations are 'doing you a favour', so bad feeling with the media will mean that you won't be able to get your good news across.

Not too long

The basic release should be no more than one side of an A4 sheet. If it is more than this, then you have probably included too much detail or made your release too complex. Journalists who want more information will contact you. If you have to run to more than one side of A4, put 'more' or 'm/f' (more follows) at the bottom right-hand corner of the page. Staple the top left-hand corner. Any OfSTED inspection release should have attached a copy of the inspection summary. Do not follow the example of a successful school in the South, where the headteacher responded to a local paper's request by suggesting that they could buy a copy of the full report for £2.50. Strangely, the lavishness of OfSTED's praise was somehow lost in the eventual news item. Send the report, free, by first-class post or drop it in to the news offices if they want it. A good write-up makes any time, trouble or cost worthwhile.

Rounding off

After you have told the story, write 'END' and underneath include an invitation to visit the school. If you are not sending photographs, offer some suggestions for pictures: an environmental project, for example. Newspapers like a good, still picture with people in it. Radio will want a mixture of sounds, and television will want sound, movement and colour. Once you have written the release, ask someone else to look at it constructively. Does it get the message across?

Pictures

'A picture is worth a thousand words.' Pictures are about people, which is what the news organizations want to put across. The number of photographers on local newspapers has fallen over the years. Those who remain will be sent on the stories which are most newsworthy. You can help get your school into this category by trying to save the newspaper time and money. This is an opportunity for your creativity! The trick is to get yourself noticed. A selection of people smiling and shaking hands and receiving trophies does not generally make for a good photograph, especially if it is staged. Spontaneity and action are the order of the day. Teachers standing up and talking to a class are also a 'turn-off'. Children's activities and achievements are much better, especially if they are at the top of a mountain, whitewater rafting, winning a race or doing voluntary work in the community. It is helpful to think how you would *like* the school to be portrayed. What image do you want to put forward – one which is staid and unimaginative, or one which is activity based, wide-ranging, exciting and unusual?

You do not need a professional photographer or a professional camera. A good-quality general camera, used properly, can take more than adequate photographs of a standard acceptable for local newspapers. In the past, black and white photographs were preferred by the press, but nowadays colour photographs are usually fine. You might check this with the newspaper. Basic rules include making sure that the people are in focus, the lighting is good and the photograph has a suitable composition. Always take many more photographs of an activity than you will possibly need. For every twenty you throw away, one may be usable.

Unsurprisingly, radio stations do not really need photographs, and schools which ring them up asking if the photograph has been used – yes, this too has happened – will be remembered, but for the wrong reasons. However, if you have sent photographs to other news organizations, send one to the radio station too, with the release, as it does add to the impression created in the journalist's mind. It may tip the balance in favour of publication.

Do not expect to get your photographs back!

Follow-up

If nothing appears, or if you have not been contacted after a few days, follow up with a telephone call to the journalist or newsdesk. This is not to berate the editor, but it is always useful to know why a release has not been used. You may find that a story has been prepared or is in the process of being written. News organizations always have a stock of stories which they may 'hold over' for a day or two as 'fillers' or a 'timeless piece'. These are rather unflattering titles for an item which is good enough for publication but which does not need to be printed or broadcast on the day the release is received.

These guidelines are no guarantee of success, but do not be discouraged. If you use these tips, you know you will be putting forward news from your school in a style which is most likely to attract the eye of the journalist and so stand the best chance of getting published.

Why news releases are rejected

You don't have to work for a PR agency to get your material in print or on the air. In fact, many of the releases that are thrown away come from PR agencies which haven't been doing their job properly. Stick to the ground rules above and you won't go far wrong.

If your release falls into any of the three areas below, it is thrown out straight away. Check that your release jumps these following hurdles.

Your school is outside the news organization's editorial area

Newspapers and broadcasting stations have editorial areas. If your school is over the line, then it doesn't exist as local news. However, it may be that part of your school's catchment is within the editorial area although the buildings are not. The release will need to be written so that the angle of the children living within the editorial area is stressed.

The news is too old

'Old' in news terms can be variable. There is often no need to mention dates or times when you write a release, but if you are wanting to comment on an issue which was in the newspaper the previous week, this is likely to be too late. If you are commenting on something which was on the radio earlier in the week, this too is likely to be too late. Radio stations have hourly bulletins and therefore hourly deadlines. An urgent story can be written up in a basic fashion for transmission by a journalist in a couple of minutes. Many stories will have aspects which people in particular positions will want to comment upon. The editor will want to run these 'developing' stories throughout that day and possibly leave an item overnight for transmission the next morning. Often, the various 'angles' on the story will have been covered by the station within one day. If you write in a few days later you will have missed the boat.

Weekly newspapers are at the other end of the scale, with just one chance every seven days to publish information. Find out when the appropriate deadlines are, and make sure you get material to the paper in plenty of time. If you miss out, one more week may mean that the story is out of date.

Your 'news' is not news

What you have sent in may not pass the basic test of general interest set out earlier in this chapter. There is no reason why the material should be of interest to a wider readership or audience. You might test this with friends and colleagues who are not involved with the school. If they are interested, others might be.

Action points

1   Take one of the four events you identified in Chapter 3's action points and develop a news release.
    (a) Write a short but catchy title.
    (b) Write an opening paragraph which summarizes the main point (only one!) of the release in the first sentence and then develops this in a second sentence. This should be no more than five lines. (Remember, keep things simple.)
    (c) Write a second paragraph which expands on what you have said and introduces new information. This could be why what you are saying is unusual, or relevant background material on your school or teachers/pupils.
    (d) Identify two individuals whose quotes you could include in the release. What sort of things would be best to include as a quote? Remember that the quotes should add to the content of the release, not just be self-congratulatory.
2   Take cuttings from local newspapers about educational issues and school activities in your area. Look at the tone and content. Divide the cuttings into three categories:
    (a) items which have a positive tone towards a school;
    (b) items which have a negative tone towards a school;
    (c) items of general educational interest.
        (i)   Are there any themes or 'running stories' which emerge in the cuttings?
        (ii) What types of 'good' stories appear? Does one of the local newspapers appear to be more receptive to positive educational stories? What kind of stories?
        (iii) Could someone from your school have given an appropriate comment about the items of general educational interest? Governor/chair/headteacher?

Chapter 5

Coping with crisis

How to deal with an incident that attracts
unwanted media attention. What to do in an
emergency.

Dealing with crises

The image that people have of an individual school is often shaped
by how it copes in a crisis. The crisis could be on a small scale, such
as having to close because of bad weather. Tragically, it might be
dealing with a major disaster. Ultimately, people outside the
school will usually need to be told quickly, accurately and effectively
about a situation. There is a need for people to know *relevant* information. If this is not given in a controlled and planned way, then the
crisis can become worse. Telephone lines become permanently
engaged, LEA officials are not able to make contact, inaccurate
information is issued – confusion and panic can result.

This chapter looks at some of the issues of which headteachers
and governors should be aware before a crisis occurs in order to
help them make the best of a situation. It also emphasizes that
schools should not work alone in dealing with crises. Other parties
will often have to be brought in at an early stage to assess the serious-
ness of the situation, to help manage the crisis and, in particular, to
deal with questions from the media.

Also, this chapter goes beyond the broad definition of crisis
management to encompass strategies to deal with adverse publicity
in general and issues that could affect the reputation of your school.

Crisis management for schools: an overview

'Crisis management' is a much misunderstood term. What it refers to
is a prepared plan of action which is to be implemented when something goes wrong. Although it is not appropriate for individual
schools to go to the lengths taken by some industries to deal with

crises, it is useful to devise a general policy of managing communication with the media and others when we are faced with bad news or adverse publicity. We also need to know when to hand things over to specialists in this field.

The key to effective crisis management lies in anticipating possible scenarios, preparing a plan of action, and ensuring that all likely major players know their roles. If this is done calmly and with reflection before an event, then this planning can feed through into immediate and effective action when the need arises. Where appropriate, a plan of action should be drawn up in conjunction with any 'serious incident or crisis' guidelines or procedures issued by the LEA. In practice, the headteacher, senior management of the school and the chair of governors should be familiar with any guidelines. It is helpful if all governors are formally made aware of the school crisis procedure and are updated on this from time to time. Staff also need to be aware of the crisis plan, in general, and their role in its implementation, in particular.

Crises which schools throughout the country have had to deal with in recent years include accidents on school trips involving injury to or the death of pupils and teachers, teenagers being killed out of school in a traffic accident, fires and explosions within school and the threat of serious violence or the carrying out of a violent attack on pupils and/or staff. In cases such as these there is an important psychological need for children and staff that must be catered for through provision of appropriate short-term and long-term professional counselling. It is not within the scope of this book to deal with this psychological and extremely important element of crisis management. Thorough and authoritative guides already exist on this subject (for example, Yule and Gold, 1993). Stirling Council has brought together its own terrible experiences in a handbook (Stirling Council Education Services, 1999; Lord Cullen's report on Dunblane [1996] also repays study.) Where appropriate, post-crisis support will be coordinated through the LEA.

The art of good crisis management lies in advance preparation, the call for expert assistance at an early stage, and a telling of the truth. No one likes to talk about things which have gone wrong at school, but often a school's good reputation will remain intact if the headteacher and governors take a positive approach to crisis management.

Stages of a crisis

Stage 1: the beginning

The crisis itself is the immediate issue which has to be faced, and priorities for action must be established. Communication to a range of people of what has happened and what is happening will be one of these priorities. If the incident is small-scale and the headteacher believes they have the skill and capacity to cope with the issue, then there is no need to ask for advice, but in practical terms it may be helpful to contact a designated officer or organization at this early stage. Some LEAs have a set procedure to be followed whenever the reputation of a school could be affected by an incident, and all have a procedure for emergencies. An LEA officer will guide the headteacher and chair of governors in drafting a media statement if the incident is not major, but this may also be carried out in conjunction with the police and other officials, depending on the nature of the crisis. The area officer will also liaise with other bodies and individuals as appropriate, usually in conjunction with the authority's communications unit. Non-maintained schools, of course, do not have these facilities open to them. An arrangement with a local authority or private agency is sometimes possible. Such schools may want to investigate the services available in their area.

If the police are involved in a major school-related crisis, then they will take control of communication with the media, working where appropriate with the local authority. Their task is to give relevant information to journalists, sometimes at a site close to the crisis, with regular updates on the situation. The media are the main information conduit to the wider public. The authorities then know the media have accurate and up-to-date information and not rumour or hearsay. The police will seek to manage the information flow by providing personnel involved in the crisis at news conferences. No member of school staff is forced to participate in the conference, but the police media experts will gauge the best way of presenting a crisis situation and this may involve a headteacher or chair of governors being asked to participate.

When police are involved in a school incident, legal and operational constraints individually mean that comment and interviews with media must be handled by the police. An apparently innocuous comment could land a headteacher with a writ for defamation or lead to the perpetrator of a criminal act walking free.

Some people may wonder why so much emphasis is placed on crisis management and communication. The answer comes when an organization gets its crisis management wrong. In this case, a number of things happen. In particular, incorrect information can be given out. This may say that people have been injured when they have not. It may say that everyone is safe when they are not. People need to know what is going on, but they need to be given a true picture. The wider public learns this from the media. Relatives of those involved need to be kept up-to-date personally, wherever possible. From a common-sense point of view, it cannot be right to put out incorrect information, whether it be a deliberate lie or conjecture. The damage to the organizations involved – schools, the LEA and so on – and their image will be much greater if a cover-up is suspected than if confirmed facts are given out only when a situation becomes clearer.

In a major incident, within a very short space of time hundreds of journalists with camera crews, photographers and microphones may be converging on your school. Having assistance from public relations (PR) and communication experts to manage the media presence takes this pressure away from others directly involved in the crisis. This allows them to keep their minds on dealing with the crisis itself. You must be in no doubt that, if you think the journalist will go away without a story, then that journalist will get information somehow. This may well be unreliable information, and possibly detrimental, not just to the image of the school but to the way people within the school see themselves, both staff and pupils. This has a human consequence. It is not just about 'image'.

At this early stage, there are often sketchy details about the crisis that has occurred. If there has been a coach accident, how many people are involved, how many are injured, where have they been taken? This information may be confused in the beginning. Details will usually be provided by the police or other emergency services direct to the media even at the early stage. Journalists regularly telephone fire brigade, police and ambulance headquarters with 'check calls' to get information about crimes and other incidents of interest which can be written up into a story. This is when details of a major incident can be first released. Sometimes the emergency services will contact the media organizations directly. People living nearby to the scene of news events will often tip off the media. It is then up to the journalist who takes the call to verify this with the police. This method of tip-off from the public often means that the news organizations become aware that a major incident is taking place even before the police arrive on the scene and before initial verification material is recorded on the police computer.

The news only has to be broadcast once, typically on local radio, for a media avalanche to take place. The initial broadcast is made. The first journalist to pick up the story contacts the national news-desk of their organization, and one of the journalists there will gauge the incident's relative importance to the rest of the day's news and may choose to send a reporter with technical support to the scene. 'Technical support' in this sense may mean a satellite truck with operator, camera operator, sound operator and photographers. If a freelance journalist is listening to the broadcast, they will verify the details and tip off other local media and the national newspapers and news agencies. Within a few minutes of a major incident taking place, all local media and the national media may have been made aware of it, and from then the news agencies, such as the Press Association, will have put out to their subscribers the first details. This can translate into a news flash on television or radio, instant publication on teletext and Internet services and inclusion in the next print run of the newspaper.

Keeping the media informed about what is going on enables management of the flow of information. In short, if the media are given, and publish, up-to-date information (especially on radio, with a fast-developing incident), then people will turn to the local radio for news on the latest situation. In talking to the media, the police, the headteacher or other staff will reach thousands and possibly millions of people for a major incident. Dealing effctively with the media can clear lines of communication and allow those involved in the incident itself to get on and deal with their expert role. If the emergency services and local authority information managers take a proactive role with the media, then the flow of information about a situation can be controlled. In police operations, this is often very important not just for legal reasons but also because of the delicate nature of some of the information being handled. Ground rules will also be made clear to journalists. But there must be a reasonable amount of give and take. One particular journalist may be given 'privileged' access to (for example) an operations room, on the basis that the film footage and information they get is 'pooled' with all the other news organizations. In this way, all the journalists obtain shots and interviews they would not normally expect and the operations room is not unduly disturbed by the presence of just one camera and reporter.

It is generally accepted that schools, with LEA and emergency service support, need to respond swiftly to media inquiries about the crisis. When facts are thin on the ground, it is tempting to say, 'No comment.' When this appears in print or on the air as 'the head-teacher refused to comment on . . .' this immediately tends to portray the wrong message of 'something to hide'. If the media are told that a statement is being prepared, provided it is produced quickly, this will often be sufficient to deal with the initial demand for information.

Certainly, there is a considerable amount of control in crisis management both in communication with media and in dealing with the crisis itself. In short, it is a way of effective communication which, in turn, means that the people and organizations dealing with the incident come out of it in a positive light. Crisis management and communication of what is going on has no bearing on how people actually use their expertise to deal with the crisis but are designed to maintain order and sensitivity during what is, for many people involved, a crucial, frightening and emotional time.

Stage 2: the developing crisis

As the crisis and its coverage develops, more details will become available. It is important throughout the course of the crisis that people are honest and truthful about what has been happening. In a serious incident, individuals who are to make statements to the media will usually be briefed by police as to what to say and what not to say, and why. They will also be 'protected' in the news con-ference, if need be by the communications experts, to make sure that what is said is correct and that the speaker is not 'forced' to develop areas of their statement which are not appropriate. This may be for legal reasons or for what police call 'operational' reasons. If a police negotiation is under way, then the information put out on the broadcast media may be picked up by the wrong people. Also, for reasons of evidence, a significant fact may be withheld from the media.

Just as details of a crisis at the outset may be sketchy, so there will usually come a stage in a crisis or major incident when nothing is actually happening which can be given to journalists. In order to make a story, the journalist will need to be given regular updates or told of developments in the situation in order to refresh what is appearing in print or 'on the air'. In this case, police typically will not release all the details they have about a situation at once. They can hold some information back which can then be given to journalists at a later news conference. So long as all the journalists receive the information at the same time, this is seen as a legitimate way of managing information by both the police and journalists. In this way, the journalists get their regular official updates on the situation and the police make sure they are able to hold the journalists' attention and so put forward information in the way they would like.

Stage 3: conclusion of the crisis

This may come quite swiftly in some cases with the arrest of an individual. In the case of a traffic accident, for example, final details of casualties may be released, but this may mark the beginning of a 'winding-down' period as far as the media are concerned. Usually, the national media will be present during a crisis and leave immediately afterwards. But the local media are different. Local media represent the feelings, mood, anger, sadness, beliefs and compassion of people in the area. If they did not, people would not buy the newspapers or listen to the broadcasts. The local media will often continue with the after-effects of a crisis story long after the nationals have gone away. They will want to focus on how individual local people have been affected by a tragedy and how a school has come to terms with what has happened. Usually, these stories are followed up in a sympathetic and constructive manner by local news organizations. Once again, although the police may no longer be co-ordinating the news management issues, there may be continued support through the LEA or other agencies.

What can schools do for themselves?

Much of what has been written in this chapter has been to do with the role of people and organizations other than the school in dealing with a crisis within the school. It is important to be able to draw on the experience and resources of others, and in most cases it will be immediately apparent when this has to be done. But schools do need to be alive to the fact that some issues will appear in the media which, although not a life or death matter, are not flattering. On such occasions, a response is needed to put the school's case.

Governors with professional media experience can be of particular help in this regard. Governors who think they are experts simply because they have been interviewed by a journalist should be brought back down to earth! Essentially, there are two types of 'bad' news which schools could be expected to deal with for themselves: first, situations which could be predicted as possible areas for negative comment about the school; and, second, those which could not. This section does not deal with the major incidents or crises discussed elsewhere but purely with the issues which can be handled 'in-house'.

Planning is the key to dealing successfully with the foreseeable crisis. Equally, it is the key to laying down the framework for handling the less predictable incidents.

Possible problem areas

There is a wide range of issues which could attract negative coverage in the media. Sponsorship in schools, relations with nearby residents, dissatisfaction with staff or the school as a whole, a suspended teacher or a negative OfSTED report are just a ew of the more familiar examples. For an item to appear in the media it does not need a majority of parents to bombard the offices of the news organization with letters and phone calls. Just one parent or pupil can set the ball rolling.

Normally, the school will be approached for a comment prior to publication or broadcast. You may disagree totally with the point being made and regard it as a complete misinterpretation of an issue. If you have thought about the issue beforehand as a possible problem area and devised an overall response, this can be introduced if the predicted problem area becomes an issue.

Who is involved

Identify members of staff who have skills and positions appropriate to the situation. These are typically the headteacher and/or deputy, with perhaps another member of staff with responsibility for publicity, and the chair of governors, together with a governor who has broad experience of dealing with the media (and getting good results!).

Role play and media training

Essentially, the pros and cons of various responses are discussed and rehearsed, and the best one is selected. When MPs and other politicians are interviewed on television, especially near election time, they will have been grilled in role play by members of their own media unit. This is a helpful way of evaluating potential strategies and is discussed further in Chapter 6. Practising these communication skills with colleagues will make you more able to respond effectively.

If the governors adopt a positive attitude towards the media, then the matter of dealing with possible negative media comment will be addressed as an important issue as a matter of course. Coupling this with the good news stories which will be coming out of your school because of the proactive stance on publicity, the school's reputation will be enhanced, pupils and staff will feel more positive about their achievements, and the local media will think more highly of you as a source of professional comment about issues on education in general and your school in particular.

Guidelines for crisis management

Some key rules need to be followed and are set out below.

Tell the truth

Tell the truth as you see it. Ensure that the audience understands that you can talk about those things which you know or believe to be true. Everyone involved in a crisis has their own distinct perspective. Show that you respect other people's perceptions, even if you disagree with them.

Don't say 'no comment'

'No comment' sometimes means 'We have something to hide.' It always sounds as if you have something to hide. If you have been asked not to make a media statement by police, then tell the journalist that you are unable to comment because all media inquiries are being handled by the police. If you cannot say anything, then tell the journalist why you cannot say anything. You can produce a short 'holding piece' of a few lines which you can say will be released in, say, 15 minutes. It is important to be in control but also to let the journalist know what is likely to develop. It also tends to be self-defeating to tell the journalist that 'this is not a story'. Such a comment is likely to make the journalist more determined to run the story.

Don't get out of your depth

It may be tempting to keep management of a crisis 'in-house'. After all, it is you who runs the school and it is you who are meant to be the expert on all aspects of school management. You are never just talking to the local media; they have national and international contacts. An apparently innocuous story can easily be blown up and sold to the national media if the first contacts are not handled properly. In a crisis, it will be clear that LEA or other support may need to be brought in at an early stage. But when a journalist first telephones you, this may not be so apparent. It is important to use what expertise is available. If for no other reasons, there may be legal considerations to be taken into account when dealing with the naming of individuals and schools.

Different media, different needs

A short, holding release about the incident will keep journalists happy for a while. Radio stations will usually want a voice saying what is in the release. Voices are their pictures. You will sometimes see on television and hear on the radio people reading a statement from a piece of paper. This is in order, but you should try not to sound too much as if you are reading. This may come across as sounding unauthentic. If you are unhappy about reading the piece, do not feel pressured to do so.

Keep the contact going

During a major incident, the regular feeding of journalists with information about the situation will show them that the authorities understand their needs and are catering for them. The media are your route to the wider public, so it is best to keep them on board and provide them with the information you want to give them. They may not use it, but if you produce new angles for them to report on then you have some control over the reporting.

Stick to the facts

Do this and you cannot be accused of not telling the truth. It prevents harmful conjecture and second-guesses more detailed analysis of the incident. During the initial stages of a crisis many rumours will be flying around. Do not use rumour itself as a means to fuel further rumours.

Could you have planned for this event?

Does this event fall into the category of problem areas which could have been anticipated? Did you anticipate it? Did you act on it? If the answer is 'yes' to all three questions, you have a good idea about what is going to happen from the point of view of the media and you have responses to the concerns that you expect to be raised. You may even have pre-empted any negative publicity by putting out a release with an upbeat positive message in the first place and with robust answers to negative aspects. You also have direct access to parents through their children and via newsletters. You can say precisely what you want to say without fear of any mis-reporting. Also, your staff would prefer to hear the message coming from you first rather than from the newspaper. Clearly, there is no point in covering up something which is fundamentally wrong. In such an event, always admit that this is the case. You will be given credit for understanding people's concerns. No one believes that institutions are perfect – least of all schools! Indeed, everyone believes that they know exactly what is wrong with their local school. After all, going to school is something we all know about. It is therefore usually a good idea to comment on some areas for improvement. It often implies that you are trying to make a good school even better. However, in general, there is little point in deliberately drawing attention to negative aspects. If the answer to all three questions is not 'yes', you can do better – but you may need to get down to some serious planning!

Evaluation

After the immediate crisis is over and things begin to return to a state of some order, it is useful to debrief those involved. County emergency plans undergo simulation exercises on a regular basis but that is all that they are – simulations. Everyone dreads putting emergency plans into action for real, but that is the only way in which they can be truly tested. You can be sure that after a major incident there will be an extensive debriefing and evaluation. For the less serious incident or report which merits limited outside involvement, an evaluation by the senior management team is helpful so that lessons are learned. It may be useful to ask an independent person to help in a debriefing in order to produce a more objective review.

Some textbooks treat crisis management purely as a method of making sure that an organization's reputation remains intact. The reputation and the perception to those outside the organization is everything. Some PR consultants talk about viewing a crisis or serious incident as an opportunity. This seems to disregard human life as far as those who may have suffered are concerned and for those who will live with the memory of an incident forever. Those who work in and with schools tend to work with people, not with economic units. They see people for the individuals that they are, and it is the job of the staff to help individuals tap their talents for the benefit of the child and society in general. To view a school's or LEA's reaction to an injury to or the death of one of these people – staff or pupil – primarily as an opportunity to enhance the reputation of the school defies comment.

Action points

1   Look at the range of negative cuttings taken from the previous chapter:
    (a) Has the story been developed in the newspaper over a number of days?
    (b) Analyze the published response of the school. Is it measured, polite, positive and responsible?
    (c) Can you think of any better responses the school could have given?
2   For your own school:
    (a) Who might be members of a team to consider the school's approach to crisis management issues? Include both staff and governors.
    (b) Consider a governor training programme for dealing with the media, especially crisis management.

(c) Do you and other headteachers and deputies in other schools want training in this area? If so, identify appropriate sources.

(d) Ensure that the senior management team is aware of the content of any LEA serious incident/crisis plan for schools.

(e) Identify some issues which attracted, or might have attracted, negative publicity for your school over the past year. How was the matter handled? Could these issues have been handled differently given the guidelines in this chapter?

Chapter 6

Managing the message

How to ensure that your school gets the best possible coverage, identifying all target publications, organizations and individuals.

Media relations: an overview

At the training sessions we run on dealing with the media we are sometimes faced with governors who are angry. They are angry with newspapers and radio stations and use us as the butt for all the work of the media where things have not gone strictly according to a school's plan. We are told that they as governors and their head-teachers will never again talk to the newspapers because they have been misquoted and 'they' only look for bad news. We work on the basis that such outbursts are a cathartic release for people who believe they have been 'stitched up' by the local paper or radio/ television station. The fact that these people have turned up for a training session on how to do things properly suggests that they can be turned round. In short, they don't know how to work with the media and want to find out how.

This chapter builds on the skills and techniques that need to be developed. They are the skills that help to create and maintain a good relationship with the people who must be nurtured in order to get your positive message across. Going through the action points in the previous chapters and thinking about how to work with the media by knowing how they operate will give you an edge in your material.

Get to know a journalist

They don't all bite! Most journalists on local newspapers will be pleased to hear from a school which wants to get its publicity material into shape. They may be able to take up an invitation to visit your school and talk to the pupils as well as to you. Remember, it is also good public relations for the editor of the newspaper, or one of the journalists, to be seen as a friendly and approachable part of the community. In general, editors will weigh up all the other demands on staff time and make a decision. If you can link in an invitation for a visit with a specific story, then so much the better. Sometimes, journalists negotiate exclusive stories for their publication or broadcast organization. This does not mean that money changes hands. It is, rather, a commitment that if a particular newspaper is given details of a story before others then there is some assurance of coverage. It is an arrangement which suits both the school and the newspaper or broadcaster. The negative aspect of this sort of arrangement is that it can irritate the other media who have not been part of the 'deal'.

Editors will be more likely to free up a journalist to talk to the school if they are going to get their message across to a wide audience. This may be to a group of Year 11 students about careers, or as part of a media studies course or to a group of governors or senior staff from a number of schools. The payback for the editor is that the newsdesk is not bombarded with insignificant news items and you have a name and a face to submit news to, even though the material is subsequently passed to someone else. Any professional relationship with the media therefore needs to be mutually beneficial. Many newspapers nowadays contain special education supplements from time to time. The motive can often be financial. If a school is in the newspaper, then parents of pupils there will tend to buy the newspaper on that day. But it is also part of the newspaper's remit to reflect what is happening in the local community, and that includes school life.

A number of different media organizations will exist in your local area. If you have developed a professional relationship with just one, this may be harmful in developing wider media coverage. Try to get to know representatives from all the newspapers and broadcasting organizations that serve your catchment area.

In short, it is important to try to develop a professional relationship with the media in your area. This involves understanding their needs as well as putting yours across. It is a long-term involvement which may not yield much fruit early on. But when the media recognize that you are committed to good media relations you will see the benefits that this can bring. You may be reluctant to embark on this relationship because of some negative publicity in the past, but if you put this behind you then this can lead to better media coverage and an enhanced perception of your school.

Who do I write to?

Local media

Identify the media organizations which have an interest in your particular geographical area. This includes newspapers (free and paid-for, daily and weekly), community magazines and publications, radio and television stations. The number of radio stations in the UK has been increasing dramatically over the past few years, so make sure you have details of all the newer stations. The fact that you may read a particular newspaper or listen to one radio station does not mean that the people you want to get your message do as well. In general, BBC local radio stations tend to have more speech-based programmes which may lend themselves more easily to your news releases. However, the audience profiles of the BBC local radio stations tend to show an older listenership than those of local commercial stations. If you are trying to get a message across to parents of younger children, then the BBC local radio station may not be the best idea. However, the other side of the coin is that a publication or station with an older audience profile means that you have a higher chance of catching the grandparents!

Editorial areas

Find out the editorial areas of your local media. Look at regional and local media of nearby towns and cities. Is there any overlap of their editorial area with your catchment area? If so, you have a good argument for including those organizations in your distribution list. Issues which affect the children will also affect their family, so this increases the number of people involved and, as a result, the strength of the story.

Editor or journalist?

News releases are usually addressed impersonally to 'The Editor'. There is no harm in sending the same release to, say, the Education Correspondent or Features Department. It is helpful to include the name of the person if sending to anyone other than the Editor. It is true that different journalists would be looking for different aspects or 'angles' in a story, so a release that is rejected by the newsdesk may be of interest to the Education Correspondent.

The way a newsroom works means that releases rejected by one department are also considered by the same person for other openings in the organization. However, this should not always be left to chance. If there are different angles for different departments, try to bring these out early in the release and in the title, and so send 'tailor-made' releases to the individuals concerned.

Deadlines

Find out the deadlines of the news organization. Do not run up tight to the deadlines or your news release will be, at best, held over for the following edition or rejected as being out of date by the time the next edition appears. For a weekly paper, try to get releases delivered at least three days before the paper is printed.

News directory

Compile a news directory for use by the individuals in charge of news and publicity. These details need to be kept up to date as media jobs have a high turnover. Often a change in people's positions will be clear if you read the newspapers, listen to the radio or watch the television. It is always worthwhile checking that your facts are correct – and hope the journalist does the same!

News-gathering techniques

News organizations use a wide range of methods to obtain local news. In many cases, news does not just happen; it is created or generated by the newspaper or broadcast station itself. In effect, this is the media being proactive and actively looking for people's views on a particular situation, rather than an event taking place and their then reporting on it. The value of a story to a news organization will often depend on how it can be portrayed in a particular medium. As mentioned elsewhere, newspapers like pictures, dramatic not posed, whereas radio stations like sounds and television likes movement and colour.

Below are some of the ways in which a local news organization will find out about what is going on in its area.

By a freelancer (otherwise known as a 'stringer')

This can be either an individual journalist or a local news agency. The freelancer 'finds out' about what is happening, interviews people, writes up the story and then sells it to the news organization. If you are tempted to use a freelance journalist who offers to 'do your PR for free', then you must check the basis on which he or she is intending to operate. The stringer is usually paid for each story sold to a news organization by that newspaper or broadcast station. Newsrooms are clearly under no obligation to buy stories from stringers and, with the editor's budget as tight as the headteacher's, journalists may be under pressure not to buy such stories. Be sure you are not being used to supplement someone's income behind your back. Certainly, if a professional journalist writes the release for you, then there is some chance that all the required material will be there in the correct format and layout, but newsrooms will not want to pay for stories which really should have been provided free of charge by the school itself. If the school does employ an outside expert, ensure that the journalist is not being paid twice – once by the school and later by the news organization.

The recruitment of a journalist (freelance or not) as a governor can be an asset to the governing body when it comes to publicity. Even if he or she guides someone else in drawing up and implementing a public relations policy, the expertise and contacts are likely to be invaluable.

A local angle on a national story

This is a common way of generating local news. It is what makes the local media different from the national. The national news is the base for the story but it is developed through contacts within the area. For example, in a national story about high stress levels for teachers, the local media responds by interviewing leaders of local teaching unions and headteachers. They may have contact details of a teacher who has taken early retirement through stress and who is happy to talk about this.

Similarly, a school can take a proactive approach to this. If there is a national story regarding education which you would like to comment on, you may telephone newsdesks direct to offer them your views. The difference between the giving of views by headteachers and governors, as opposed to the general public doing so, is that people with formal positions in schools have the standing to make comments. Their views are seen as those of the school and not those of an individual – with the attendant risks.

Journalists' contacts

A journalist may get in touch with an individual who appears in the news from time to time to ask if there is anything of 'interest' going on. Both know the score. The paper or news bulletin needs to be filled and, especially in the summer when many political stories tend to die down, journalists can often be scratching around for news stories. You, as a governor or headteacher, may be able to use this as an opportunity to push for some positive PR for your school. You are in the driving seat in this case. The journalist is implying that there may be some difficulty in obtaining all the stories which are needed from usual sources and that now is the time to put out some 'feelers' to see if there are any stories which should have been covered. There are slow news days, when items which might have been rejected at another time appear in print or on the air.

One of the criteria for being contacted like this is how well you come over in print, on the radio or on television. If you have proved to be a competent performer in the past, you are more likely to be contacted either for a chat with the journalist about any developments in education and your school in particular, or asked to comment on a relevant national story. Journalists will also note in their 'contacts book' or store in their memory how well you come over in the media. A positive impression here will do wonders for publicity for your school.

The running story

News is often created through a mixture of opinions about a specific matter. Because a range of people will have different opinions about matters, such issues can become running stories, especially popular during the summer months when, typically, there is less news around. Where there is no clear resolution to a local issue, these topics can be resurrected or updated and a fresh set of opinions found. Also a story can be 'moved on' by journalists who seek out reactions to other points of view. In fact, a debate is taking place within the pages of a newspaper or on the air. In such a debate, the arguments may be developed over a number of days or editions of a paper or over a series of bulletins. Typically, a story which has run on radio with developments throughout the day will be packaged together either in a feature (2 to 3 minutes long) or as a 'wrap' for the news. A wrap may be 40 seconds in length. Clips from various participants in the story are sandwiched between an introduction from the journalist, links between the sound clips and a final statement from the journalist.

Emergency services

Journalists make calls several times a day to the press offices of the emergency services. With schools in particular, if certain especially sensitive areas are involved, details are either sometimes not revealed to the media or editors may be told about a situation and asked to respect a news blackout. Responsible editors will always respect a request for a formal news blackout. It is in their long-term interest. They will see and respect the wider consequences of not publishing or broadcasting details of particular events. In return, they will properly look for cooperation from the emergency services when reporting future incidents.

In general, just as there is no right to publicity about something, there is equally no right to stop something being published. The exceptions tend to be court injunctions where there is a prima facie case in law against the publication of certain material. Legal remedies are available to plaintiffs after publication but, if the story is essentially true, then there is little that can be done.

Diary items

These are events which happen on a particular day and where notice is sent to the news organization in advance. These items will often be held until the day of the event itself. It is useful to send news items such as this about a week in advance. This gives journalists a chance to prepare an item in advance and to allow forward planning for deployment of staff.

Formal meetings and agendas

A council meeting agenda may be long and contain dozens of items. Newsrooms will usually receive a copy of all agendas for the full council meetings and those of the committees and sub-committees if the editor requests this. When the documents are received by a newsroom they are usually scanned for items which have not been raised in the media before. In these cases, the journalist may write a story there and then, based on the agenda and a report. There may be an interview with a council officer, councillor or other individuals with a view on the matter. That item may be published ahead of the meeting, with an updated item on the day of the council meeting itself.

Journalists find council agendas useful because they can provide several stories from one source: first when the agenda is released; another on the day of the meeting, and finally a piece reporting the outcome of the meeting. Proposed school closures and the replacement of crossing patrols are emotive issues which can keep the pot boiling for several months. Although such news is usually at council level or equivalent, there may be occasions when an item under consideration by an individual governing body merits wider circulation. This will be even more true of a collective governing body in an Education Action Zone.

Tip-offs

Tip-offs may originate from a freelancer or from someone who has come to hear of an issue. As with any of the issues here, they can be a double-edged sword. 'Leaks' of confidential or sensitive items may assist one side of a debate, but reaction can be unpredictable. Some newspapers and radio stations actively encourage readers and listeners to contact them with possible stories, ranging from accidents and explosions to redundancies and discontent. The sources are often anonymous and may be disgruntled students, parents, neighbours or employees. If a member of staff contacts the media with a story of unrest in a school, the journalist may or may not know their name. They are, of course, not obliged to identify their source to you. If this happens, it might be classifiable as a crisis which needs an appropriate strategy (see the previous chapter). Refusal to speak to a journalist may fuel suspicion and result in a more critical report.

Comments made 'off the record'

Off-the-record statements can mean different things to different people. Such statements are designed to give journalists some sensitive information in order to help them understand a situation, but on the basis that this information is not reported. It helps them see the wider picture. It may be reasonable for a headteacher or governor to expect such off-the-record statements to be kept confidential, but it is important that this ground-rule is established at the outset. You also have to be confident that the journalist you are dealing with is able to respect this, and that their understanding is the same as yours.

Certainly, when you first have dealings with the media, it is generally advisable to work on the assumption that anything you say may be reported in a story. By all means give background details. This will be very helpful to the journalist in writing the story, but be aware that the journalist is listening to everything you are saying. If you mention something as a throwaway remark, then it may be reported.

This is where the issue of a continuing professional relationship with journalists and their news organizations pays dividends. The more dealings you have with journalists, the more you will get to know them and the way they work. Some you will grow to trust more than others. With some you will be confident, knowing that anything you say off the record will be treated as confidential in reporting the story. You are, after all, helping the journalist understand the broader context.

Evaluation of media coverage

Dealing with the media takes time, effort and expense. Major organizations need to monitor the quantity and quality of coverage they are getting and compare this to the amount spent in obtaining it. The issue is not just about how much publicity is obtained, but measuring the effect of that coverage as well. In evaluating media coverage, companies will be measuring changes in people's perceptions of their own brands and individual products together with those of their competitors. None of this publicity takes place in a vacuum. Other companies are carrying out their own promotional campaigns which will affect the way people see the first company's products. Significant amounts of money are spent on monitoring promotional campaigns.

For schools, for funding and organizational reasons, the situation is necessarily somewhat different. However, the overall goal remains the same. Some measure needs to be taken of the success or otherwise of the promotional methods used by the school.

What has to be measured is whether people's attitudes have changed in a positive way towards our school as a result of the effort we have put into dealing with the media.

Media log

A school needs to keep a log of published material both with press cuttings and copies of broadcast media items. While strictly speaking the broadcast is the copyright of the broadcasting organization concerned, no objection will normally be raised to recording a copy 'off air' for your archive purposes. Indeed, it is likely that your school's off-air recording agreement already covers this. You should be aware that broadcasting organizations will not always be keen to produce copies of material which have been transmitted, but even if this is possible then there is usually a cost involved. The time which is taken in locating a particular item from an original, master tape or copy, together with the transfer onto a cassette or VHS tape, usually makes the cost prohibitively expensive. It is much better to try to catch the item when it first appears. Transcripts of broadcasts are also generally not made. Journalists will usually give an indication to you of when an item is likely to appear in print or on the air but no guarantee can be given. Where and when your item appears will depend on other items of news that day, the time or space available and the type of story.

A school might nominate one of its governors to perform both the logging role and the contact role in media relations. This centralizes and rationalizes the practice of a school's PR policy and enables specialist expertise to be developed.

Measurement

A crude measure is the number of column centimetres or seconds broadcast. But such a technique does not take into account factors such as circulation (both in size and make-up for newspapers), the day the item appeared, or the time and length for broadcast items. A piece which is broadcast on radio news at seven or eight o'clock in the morning will reach many more listeners than one on the same station at eight o'clock in the evening. On the other hand, an item broadcast on a television news programme at half past six in the evening will generally reach far more people than an item at the same time in the morning.

If the school takes out advertisements, it is likely to be difficult to conclude what factor has really influenced people's views – the advertisements or the articles. Are the people you reach in the newspaper or on the radio and television the people you really want to talk to? Remember the different publics described in Chapter 3. Measuring output is a complicated matter.

For schools, the advanced and expensive monitoring and evaluation techniques employed by major organizations are generally inappropriate. The school has a good basis on which to measure the success of its media coverage closer to home: pupils, staff and parents. Good coverage is likely to result in greater motivation for pupils and a similar boost in morale for staff. It can be useful to compare and monitor such elements as behaviour, attendance, examination/extra-curricular success and the general 'feel-good' factor.

Feedback from parents is clearly useful in gauging the success of dealings with the media. More formal qualitative and quantitative research methods are also available to schools, such as questionnaires and discussion or focus groups. The depth of evaluation which a school undertakes will be dependent on the time, effort and expense it is willing to commit.

For many schools, the simple file of media cuttings and tapes will suffice, and this is a practical but basic way of examining the effectiveness of the media work that has been put in.

A word of warning

This book is primarily aimed at governors and headteachers. In each chapter, you have been encouraged to contact the media with newsworthy items. Please do this! The caveat is that, if news releases are sent out and contact with the media made, this is on an official basis, on behalf of the school. Because of this, the school needs to make sure that one person is in charge of publicity. Invitations, as in this chapter for example, for governors to contact the media are intended for the governor designated to deal with publicity, if there is one. It is essential that the school and governing body speak with one voice and have a channel through which to direct media comment. While there is nothing to prevent individual governors talking to the media in their official capacity, they should be aware of the long-lasting difficulties that this can create both in dealing with a particular issue and in creating tension within the governing body itself. Sticking to an agreed and delegated system ensures a planned and coordinated series of messages to develop and enhance your school's reputation.

Action points

1   Identify all the media organizations in your area and draw up a media directory for your school containing:
    (a) The contact details of any journalists in these organizations with special responsibility for education issues and the name of the editor.
    (b) Find out about their deadlines and how they would like news submitted to them.
    (c) Do they look for anything in particular when news items are submitted to them?
2   Arrange for a journalist to come to your school to see how the school operates. Think of a newsworthy item to link in with the visit. Can the journalist give a talk to the children and meet with some governors?
3   Watch out for some national stories which could have a local angle worked in. Complex educational stories from the *TES* need to be able to be explained in a simpler form. Remember to avoid jargon.
4   Start a media log. Remember that any cuttings and photographs can be included in a Governors' Annual Report (with permission from the newspaper).

Chapter 7

In the front line

How to appear at your best when the media
want to interview you.

It can happen at any time. The telephone rings and she's on to you, there's no escape. 'You'd like to come and interview me? . . . Yes, this morning would be fine . . . about an hour? . . . OK, see you then.' Sixty minutes of fretting to go. What if she asks me this or that? I can't possibly . . . I'm not feeling too well now and I'm too busy, perhaps I'll get Pat to do it. The internal dialogue of self-doubt goes on. Sounds familiar? It's not surprising given that the vast majority of headteachers and governors don't really know what to expect when a journalist rings up and it's probably easier not to think about it. But talking to a journalist need not be something to be endured.

Being interviewed

You may be asked to talk about any manner of things. Chapter 6 gives an idea of the range of stories a journalist may be pursuing. You may have been phoned up to talk about issues contained in a news release which has been sent out, but you could be asked for a comment on either a national issue or on a specific local matter. In fact, journalists will normally brief you on the telephone on subjects they want to cover. They may well ask you if there are other things you would like to add at the end of the interview. You may offer a better news angle for the journalist this way. Journalists will always remember when someone is 'a good talker', and these people will undoubtedly be borne in mind for future comment.

If you are telephoned for a comment, it is perfectly acceptable to ask for a little time if you need to confirm a particular fact or put a holding statement together. But be aware that, although a telephone interview may appear informal, it does not alter the fact that your comments are 'on the record', so you will need to be careful in framing your responses. The fact that you are not speaking to someone face to face sometimes makes people a little too relaxed and can lead to 'inappropriate' comments being made.

Feeling nervous is a perfectly natural response. If you are being interviewed on the radio you are speaking to one person – that is, the journalist or the programme presenter – and you are speaking to that person alone. Radio is a very personal medium. Broadcasters are trained to talk as if there were only one person listening. Because of this a rapport is built up between presenter and listener.

Journalists, whether they be from newspapers, radio or television, all have an interest in your coming over in the best way possible. It does not make sense for them to make you look foolish. Not only will you not talk to them again, but it will reflect back on the news organization. The readers, listeners or viewers will think that the journalist cannot do their job properly. That is something they do not want! The purpose of an interview is to explore a particular topic of the journalist's choosing, to obtain more information, and often to consider how it relates to other people's views. Media organizations have a duty to present accurate and fair information. It is the journalist's job to ensure that this is done properly.

Do not expect to have your 5-minute interview printed in full. A number of people may well have been interviewed in preparing a story and your contribution may be condensed to perhaps two or three lines or 20 seconds of sound. People who have been interviewed sometimes complain that the 'best bits' have been left out. Once the interview is concluded it is the job of the journalist to piece together the story or article in as seamless a way as possible. The journalist will take an overview of what you have said together with the views of everyone else. Not all the issues discussed in an interview can be covered in one general item, and it is for this reason that some comments will not be used.

General advice for interviews

Before the interview

1 *Prepare a number of main points:* You will want to make a number of key statements about the topic you have been asked to discuss. Think about these in advance and how you might best get them across.

2 *Make notes:* Definitely not a speech! The notes are an aide-memoire with which you can refresh your memory just before the interview. Think about the possible questions the journalist might ask and what your response might be.

3 *Facts and figures:* Have these to hand for the interview. You will feel more confident and the interview will flow more smoothly. A good performance is likely to mean that future releases will be viewed more favourably. Journalists like to interview people who produce good copy or audio.

4 *What is the journalist looking for?* It is not generally a good idea to ask the journalist for the questions before the interview, although they should tell you in advance the general areas they want to cover. To ask for the questions is likely to give the journalist a bad first impression, although it is legitimate and positive for you to ask for the subject areas. Even if the journalist is quite specific in advance about the questions they say they will ask, they will sometimes slip in an extra question in the actual interview. The journalist will want to probe the points you are putting forward, not so much to trip you up as to see if what you are saying stands up to examination from a 'devil's advocate'. Giving you a series of questions in advance therefore does not allow the development of particular topics. It implies that, whatever you say, the next question has already been decided. The journalist's role is to act in a critical capacity and to put the questions that people who do not take your view might ask. This cannot be done with a pre-arranged set of questions. If you have been told the subject area to be covered, you should be able to put yourself in the shoes of people who have a different view. This should help you to think of ways of rebutting any negative questions from the journalist.

5 *Any special requirements?* Ask the journalist before they come to the school what they would like for pictures and sound, and make arrangements for this to happen. The better the impression you can make, the higher up the list you go for future interviews.

At the interview

1 *Don't read from a script:* Whether the interview is for print or broadcast, it is not a good idea for you to read direct from something you have prepared. The only exception to this is for prepared legal statements, Even then, although text is read

verbatim, the person reading knows they have to address the cameras and microphones and will make the effort to sound as if they are not reading. When these items are included in news bulletins, the news presenter or reporter makes it clear that the person about to speak is reading from a script. If you have made extensive notes, it is probably best to turn these over or put them in a drawer, as you will be tempted to refer to them and read from them.

2 *Keep the message clear and short . . . :* Don't blur the message with lots of statistics: 80 per cent is better expressed as four out of five, 48 per cent is 'nearly half'. You can give statistics to the journalist in their written form, and they can work these into their piece, if they wish, as tables, graphs or a short sentence. Try to be to the point and answer the question put. People who have had a lot of experience at being interviewed can turn questions around and say precisely what they want to say without answering the interviewer's question. Sometimes, they can do this without anyone realizing that they haven't answered the question! But if you have something newsworthy to say which you genuinely believe in, you should not be afraid of what the interviewer has to say. If you have developed a professional relationship with the journalist, you will have some idea how the interview will go.

3 *. . . and simple:* Avoid jargon and complicated language. Remember that when people listen to the radio they have only one chance to understand what has been said. If that is missed, then they cannot go back to check what was said. News producers know this, and will try to make sure that whatever clips of interviews they put out are clear, short and simple. Jargon is seen as 'noise' in communication theory. It prevents the real message getting from the sender (that is, you) to the intended receiver (the reader, listener or viewer).

4 *Be interested in what you say:* If you are not interested in or enthusiastic about your topic, why should anyone else take notice? If you sound bored when you are on the radio, you will not get your message across.

5 *Ensure you are not interrupted:* Phones should be switched off or diverted where the interview is taking place. (Don't forget mobile phones.) Make sure people know you are not to be interrupted.

6 *Look at the interviewer:* Eye contact with the interviewer is very important. For television, the camera will be shooting at an

angle. If you suddenly look at the camera, then the shot may be ruined. It is the journalist's job, or that of the camera or sound operator, to make sure the technical equipment is working properly. Do not move closer to any microphones or speak more loudly unless you have been asked to do so. For radio, the interviewer will hold the microphone. The operators will have taken sound levels and will make sure that the recording is running normally. They will sort out any technical difficulties. For radio and newspaper interviews too, eye contact is important. It helps communication and reinforces your message.

7 *Get all your points across:* If, at the end of the interview, you have not covered all the points you wanted to mention, then say so. The information that is missing may be what is needed to help the journalist piece the item together or offer another angle to follow up.

8 *Try to relax:* Easier said than done, especially if you have not worked with the media before. If you have 'done your home-work', both on the topic and in preparing for the interview, then there is no reason why you should not have a successful interview. Watch for signs that you are nervous; be aware of them and try to avoid them. Try not to tap the table or swing around in a swivel chair. Experienced journalists will be aware of people's nervous habits and try to create an environment and atmosphere where these will not come into play. In short, the journalist will try to put you at your ease, and you should look at this as a positive and genuine move to help everyone get the most out of the interview.

What happens next?

After the interview, the journalist may want to check some facts and spellings. Television journalists and the camera operator will probably want to take some shots of particular aspects of the school, as mentioned above. The newspaper photographer will want appropriate pictures, and the radio journalist may want to get some 'atmos' (atmosphere/background school noise) to add colour to the report. Broadcast journalists may want to record an introduction or links in their report in a classroom or the playground.

When the journalist leaves, wait for the item to appear! If a journalist has taken time to talk to you (especially if they have come to see you) there is a very good chance that your story or views will appear. However, it may take up to a week or more for the item to be printed or broadcast, as news organizations will 'hold over' items which do not have to be published immediately. Often items may be used as 'fillers' when other news items are short. If this is the case, you should not feel insulted. You are getting publicity, after all!

In the main, journalists deal fairly with the public. However, people are sometimes unhappy with the way their side has been portrayed. If you feel aggrieved, then speak to the journalist and put your points across politely but firmly. If there is a genuine cause for complaint, the editor will want to put this right as soon as possible. With local media in particular, a long-term perspective should be taken by both the school and the news organization. You need to get on with the papers and broadcasting organizations in order to make sure they give you good coverage next time!

What happens in a radio or television interview

Radio

The radio journalist may arrive in a radio car or other broadcasting vehicle for a live item, but more usually the journalist will bring their own recording equipment. This may be a high-quality portable tape or cassette recorder, but increasingly it will be a professional mini-disk recorder.

After introductions and a brief scene setting, the interview will get under way. The journalist will tell you the general areas to be covered but usually not the questions, as discussed above. They will not want to hear too much from you about the topic before the recording, otherwise you will have covered many of the things you want to say and perhaps used your best lines. You will have lost spontaneity for the recording proper.

The journalist will make a test recording to make sure the equipment is working properly (they will also have tested the equipment before leaving the radio station). Usually, some form of identifier is put on the beginning of the recording, together with a comment stating that the recording is about to begin, which will be edited out later, together with the first question.

The journalist holds the microphone and will sit next to you. The microphone should be held at chest height and not moved to any extent, as this is distracting.

If you stumble over words or answer before the reporter has finished a question, you may be asked to repeat that part. This is so that the stumble can be edited out and a perfect replacement put in. You may be asked to reply to a question again for the same reason. If the reporter makes a hash of a question, they will probably stop and repeat the question. The mistake will be edited out.

The reporter is trained to maintain eye contact and to ensure that the equipment is working properly. They may nod their head from time to time to encourage you to go on. They will usually keep silent during your reply because, when a piece is taken out for the news, they will not want their voice or 'uh-huhs' included.

The reporter may be listening for certain school background noises to create atmosphere. You may be asked to be interviewed in the playground or in a classroom when some activity is taking place.

The reporter will make sure that the place where the recording is taking place does not have an echo. Because of this, it will probably be well carpeted, with furniture and possibly curtains to absorb the sound. For this reason too, if the interview is in a hall, the recording may take place close to some curtains.

The interview will probably not last more than a few minutes. At the end, you will usually be given the chance to add any extra comments. The journalist will check the technical quality of the recording by listening to just a few seconds of the tape or disc.

You will not usually be offered the chance to listen to what you have said. This is not a devious way to deny you access to your own words, but recognition that you probably do not know how you sound to others and thus how you sound on tape. Many people do not like the sound of their voice on tape. Also, the journalist will have already mentally edited the tape, and will know what items to use for the news bulletins and possibly a feature (long interview), wrap or package (series of audio clips from different people with linking passages read by the reporter). So, what you might be played might not be the piece that makes it to air. You would not expect a newspaper journalist to repeat word for word what you have said.

Once what you have said has been recorded, this is the property of the broadcasting organization, and the copyright rests with them. You will have been told when the recording has started and when it is finished, and you are deemed to have given consent for the copyright to be passed to the radio station. Normally, you have no right to demand that an item should not be broadcast.

In reality, having just given an interview, you are not in a good position to judge its quality. The journalist will know how well you have come across and, if there is any doubt about the quality of the content, your performance or technical issues, then another recording can be made. For this to happen is quite rare.

You may ask or be asked to do the interview at the radio station's studio. The procedure will be the same as for a telephone interview, the difference being the improved studio sound quality. It is generally a better idea to have your interview in studio quality sound. It stands a better chance of being broadcast and understood. Remember the 'noise' in the communication process mentioned earlier. Anything which prevents understanding of the message you are trying to get across should be avoided where possible.

You may be talking to a journalist from a local radio station but that individual has access to a wider audience. Your interview can be passed on (sold) to national news networks, BBC or independent. Even if the interview is only broadcast locally, freelance and newspaper journalists can listen in, develop and sell the story on. Be aware that once an item is in the public domain, you have limited control as to where it is seen and heard.

Television

The television interviewer goes through the same basic process as the radio reporter, but with more complexities. Instead of just one reporter in radio who performs all the journalistic and technical functions, a television crew will normally consist of the reporter, a camera operator, who will arrange lighting, and possibly a sound operator.

The camera/lighting operator will take around 10 minutes to set the machinery up. Some sound and vision balance tests are carried out. The crew will make sure lights do not reflect off windows and that their shadow does not get into the picture with mirrors and glass screens. The crew will also be aware of possible continuity problems, such as changing weather conditions and background activities.

Colours of clothes which can cause difficulties with cameras are those that are very light or very dark. Shirts and other clothes which have fine lines or checked patterns also cause problems when broadcast on television.

Be aware of the background in any television interview. If in an office, is it tidy? If outside, what is behind you – a dilapidated part of the school or a new wing? Make sure your views are heard as to where the interview should take place, and think what could be going through the television crew's mind.

You and the reporter will either be wearing clip-on microphones, or a sound operator will be holding a 'gun' microphone.

At the end of the interview, the cameraman will take some additional shots. One of these is looking back at the reporter over your shoulder, sometimes with the reporter nodding. These 'noddies' are used to help in the editing process. Another is a shot of the reporter asking the questions again, also used in editing the piece.

How to get things right

The first interview can be very daunting, especially if you don't quite know what to expect. The tips given above will help in preparing you for your first dealings with the press, radio or television. There are also schemes which can help headteachers and governors prepare to put their message across. LEA governor and school services can be lobbied to put on media training courses, just as schools can organize their own training. External consultants such as journalists and public relations experts can be bought in centrally not just to paint the broader picture, but also to offer advice personally on your media presentations. In a supportive atmosphere, a well-organized media training session can help boost your profile and your confidence. Go on recommendation. Do not just grab the first name in the Yellow Pages.

Watch out for possible bias in training programmes newspaper journalists against broadcasters, people who have worked for the BBC against other broadcasting organizations, national newspaper journalists against local newspaper journalists, and vice versa.

Training is often offered by two individuals. Try to get complementary skills from these two 'experts'; for example, those with expertise in newspapers from one and radio from the other. You do not want to pay someone to voice their own personal agenda. You will be paying them good money to provide you with the skills and insight to make sure your school gets its message across. You deserve to get the best for your school.

Chapter 8

Righting the wrong

How to complain and get redress.

Don't get too worked up

This chapter is here to help you make sense, and use, of some of the avenues open to you if you have a genuine grievance about an item which has appeared in the press or on air.

If you have turned straight to this section of the book looking for ways to exact vengeance upon or retribution from the accursed media outlet, it is probably a good idea to stand back from the situation you are in and to assess your position. You may be angry at the way an issue has been portrayed. You may believe that a journalist has taken part of an interview with you out of context. You may feel that a newspaper or broadcasting station has been too pushy in trying to get material. On the other hand, perhaps an important issue, from your point of view, has been ignored.

Don't forget, you have *your* views on a particular topic and other people have theirs. For example, people who live near to your school are likely to have a negative view of the cars which line both sides of the street – and probably the middle – at nine in the morning and three in the afternoon. Parents will have another view: that the congestion is only for a short time in the morning and afternoon, and anyway people who live next to schools should expect that sort of thing. The headteacher will want to ensure safety for pupils and be a 'good neighbour', yet not antagonize the parents, whose support is needed for good order and the efficient running of the school. The journalist will try to obtain some sort of balance within a report. It may not be the same number of words or amount of airtime given to each group, but overall, each side will probably have had its say in the report. Alternatively, the story can be balanced up over a number of editions or bulletins. You need to remember that the journalist's job is to portray the various sides to a story, not just yours. The newspaper may also be taking a stand for or against a particular issue, which will influence the way it reports things. If you find yourself in this position, do stand back and try to see the broader picture.

Remember, you may need 'friends' in the media at some stage in the future. If you alienate the local newspaper or radio station by complaining in an 'over-the-top' manner, then you may undo a lot of good work from the past and good relationships which have been built up. It is quite possible that, because you are involved in a story, you are particularly sensitive about the way it is portrayed – much more so than the average reader, viewer or listener. Try to ensure that you see things in perspective

M'learned friends

Pursuing an action for defamation can be expensive, dangerous and notoriously unpredictable. Because of this, it is not for the faint-hearted. These comments are for background information only. Libel is defamatory material which is published. This is either in written form or material which is transmitted on radio or television. Defamatory material which is spoken (not broadcast) is slander.

This is not the place for a detailed breakdown or discussion of the legal position. Suffice it to say, if an individual feels they have been defamed (or is about to be), then an initial assessment of the situation needs to be swiftly undertaken with an appropriate solicitor. The first step that may be taken is to try to prevent publication of the material which may be libellous. This would be done through dealings with the organization having published or proposing to publish the material, and possibly by an injunction. Damages may well then be sought.

One curious twist in this area is the wide variety of people who are likely to be cited in any writ. In the newspaper world, this may be the journalist who wrote the story, together with the editor, publisher and proprietor. In commercial radio, the journalist who wrote the story, the person who provided the story (a news agency, perhaps), the news editor, the programme controller, the managing director, the chairman of the company, and the organization which provided the transmitters, among others, are all seen as fair game. The list is virtually endless.

Nowadays, if individuals are defamed as part of their work, they will usually have to pursue any action for damages themselves, particularly if they are part of a public organization such as a school. However, professional associations and trade unions may be prepared to foot the bill to fight a case. This may be not just to support their member but also to gain publicity for a particular issue.

The damages can be significant (or paltry), but so can the costs. It is typical to see the costs of pursuing – or defending – a libel action escalate at a dramatic rate. It can be argued that this is out of all proportion to the damage done. The winner in the libel case may have to pay their own costs and some of the other side's, which might be £300,000, and be awarded, say, £50,000. That is a net loss of £250,000 on a case where the individual was deemed to be the victor!

Perhaps a more appropriate course of action

Most newspapers are willing to correct material which is simply wrong or from which inappropriate inference can be drawn, if it is material and relevant to the understanding of a story. They would prefer not to do this because, when the reader sees an apology, correction or clarification, there is an assumption that the newspaper has not 'done its homework', and so the reader might start to believe that the newspaper they read is not as reliable as some others. Because of this, a 'correction' may appear, without a 'correction' heading as a story, with a positive spin for the person/organization misrepresented in the previous issue. It doesn't say, 'I'm sorry, we got it wrong', from the paper, so the editor is happy and the person complaining gets a 'free plug'.

People will often have to put up with misspellings of surnames or some factual inaccuracies. Also, don't forget that your perception of a story may be different from those of most other readers, viewers or listeners. Any correction or clarification which appears typically has less prominence than the original article and in some ways draws attention to the original error. Sometimes it is a good idea just to leave well alone. So, if you know the journalist, having cultivated a professional relationship, it is likely to be helpful to mention the error, but a longer-term and positive view needs to be taken. It may be that if you are reasonable about what has appeared – that is, make your point but not kick up too much of a fuss – then you will get a good 'write-up' the next time around.

If you have a problem with a story which appears in print or on air, then discuss the matter with the journalist who has been covering the item. You can then raise this with the editor if you are not happy with the response from the journalist. It must be said that most matters are dealt with at this somewhat informal level. The publishing organization will not want to spend often significant amounts of time – and therefore money – preparing for cases which have been sent for the consideration of regulatory bodies. On the other hand, the organization will probably defend its position if it believes it has a reasonable case. If the paper or radio/television station is going to have to say it is sorry for something which has appeared, it would rather do this voluntarily – or in another way, as described above – rather than being required to do this following a ruling by a regulatory authority.

Regulatory bodies in the UK

There can be no doubt that the range of organizations that have been set up to regulate – as best they can – the output of the media can be confusing both in their acronyms – BSC, ITC, PCC, RA – and in the role they actually perform. Is there an overlap in what they do? Am I dealing with the right body? What can it do?

It is clear that in the broadcasting field it has been decided that enough is enough. At the time of writing, a White Paper on Communications has been published which foresees the sweeping away of the authorities that oversee commercial radio and television. There is a proposal to bring their remit under the auspices of a new super-regulatory body, OfCom. On top of this, OfCom would also take on the investigation of complaints against the BBC which is currently dealt with in-house. Whether these proposals come about, only time will tell.

Let's examine the roles and responsibilities of the current regulatory bodies.

The Press Complaints Commission

The Press Complaints Commission (PCC) was set up in 1991 to try to make sure that newspapers and magazines followed the letter and spirit of a code of practice. It is a voluntary body paid for by the newspaper industry. The PCC makes a big play to say it is independent from and not influenced by the newspapers which pay for its existence. In recent years, there have been calls for statutory regulation of the newspaper and magazine industry but these have so far been resisted by the legislators. The industry set up this body as a form of self-regulation in an attempt to fend off calls for statutory regulation.

The PCC deals with around 3,000 complaints each year over matters of inaccuracy, privacy, misrepresentation and harassment. The vast majority are resolved without a formal adjudication. The PCC does not deal with matters which are the subject of legal proceedings, nor does it deal with claims for compensation. It does not cost anything to make a complaint to the PCC (apart from postage) and the aim is to reach a swift and amicable settlement. The PCC says it resolves 90 per cent of the complaints received within six weeks.

There is a helpline (020-7353-3732) and a comprehensive website (http://www.pcc.org.uk). The address is: 1 Salisbury Square, London EC4Y 8JB. Full contact details are contained in Appendix 3.

Issues from the Code of Practice (December 1999) which are likely to be of interest to headteachers and governors are as follows. The authors have italicized certain parts so as to highlight areas which may lead to a difference of opinion between school and editor:

> *Section 1 (ii)*: Whenever it is recognised that a *significant* inaccuracy, misleading statement or distorted report has been published, it should be corrected promptly and with due prominence.

Matters will, presumably, hinge around the interpretation of the word 'significant'. What is significant to the school may not be deemed to be significant to the newspaper.

> *Section 2*: A fair opportunity for reply to inaccuracies must be given to individuals or organizations when *reasonably* called for.

As above, what the headteacher deems to be a reasonable request may not be viewed in the same light by the editor.

> *Section 4 (i)*: Journalists and photographers must neither obtain nor seek to obtain information or pictures through intimidation, harassment or persistent pursuit.

Section 4 (ii): They must not photograph individuals in private places without their consent; must not persist in telephoning, questioning, pursuing or photographing individuals after having been asked to desist; must not remain on their property after having been asked to leave and must not follow them.

'Private places' are deemed to be public or private property where there is a reasonable expectation of privacy. The inside of a school is likely to be regarded as a private place whereas the grounds of the school may not. The use of long-lens photography in this respect is also unacceptable to the PCC.

Section 6 (i): Young people should be free to complete their time at school without unnecessary intrusion.

Section 6 (ii): Journalists must not interview or photograph a child under the age of 16 on subjects involving the welfare of the child or any other child in the absence of or without the consent of a parent or any other adult who is responsible for the children.

Section 6 (iii): Pupils must not be approached or photographed while at school without the permission of the school authorities.

Section 6 (v): Where material about the private life of a child is published, there must be justification for publication other than the fame, notoriety or position of his or her parents or guardians.

Where the child is famous or holds a particular position, as opposed to (or in addition to) that of the parents or guardians, that will be argued as a different scenario by the press. In such cases, the PCC generally asks the press to abide by the spirit of the code and to respect the child's privacy.

Section 11 (i): Journalists must not *generally* seek to obtain information or pictures through misrepresentation or subterfuge.

Section 11 (iii): Subterfuge can be justified only in the public interest and only when material cannot be obtained by any other means.

What is 'the public interest'?

The press complaints process starts with a letter to the editor of the publication perceived to be at fault. Does the article break the PCC Code of Practice? The response you receive will determine your next move. If you are satisfied with the editor's response, fine. Otherwise you can refer the matter to the PCC. You should be aware that in starting this next stage of the complaints process, a copy of your letter to the PCC will usually be sent to the editor of the newspaper or magazine. You may wish to bear this in mind when drafting the correspondence. You should make your complaint to the PCC within one month of publication or one month after the editor replied to your initial letter of complaint. There is provision for the consideration of complaints falling outside this timescale but this is an exceptional route. In writing to the PCC you will need to send a cutting of the article or a clear copy (with the date included). You also need to send a summary of your complaint together with any related documents and correspondence. The PCC's telephone helpline can give advice in framing your complaint.

Generally speaking, you can only complain about something which relates to you or your organization. If no agreement with the editor of the newspaper or magazine can be reached, the Commission will make a judgement on the evidence submitted to it. If a complaint is upheld, the PCC will require the newspaper to print the adjudication.

The Broadcasting Standards Commission

The Broadcasting Standards Commission (BSC) was set up by Parliament through the 1996 Broadcasting Act in order to oversee standards and fairness in broadcasting. Its remit relates to all radio and television organizations transmitting within the UK. It does not just mean the BBC and ITV stations, but all commercial radio together with satellite, cable, text and digital services. Every broadcaster is required to reflect the BSC's codes on standards and fairness and privacy in its own codes of practice. The BSC is financed by a government grant, currently of around £2 million each year. The Broadcasting Act requires the BSC to consider and adjudicate on complaints. Complaints need to be made within three months of a television broadcast and six weeks of a radio broadcast, although these deadlines can change from time to time and depend on the nature of the complaint.

The BSC website (http://www.bsc.org.uk) contains full details of the workings of the Commission and guidance on the complaints procedure.

The Code of Fairness and Privacy (November 1997) is likely to be of most relevance to headteachers and governors. The code begins by requiring broadcasters to use accurate information and to make sure this isn't distorted or taken out of context. People asked to make a significant contribution to a factual programme should be given details of the nature of the programme, why they have been asked to contribute and the general areas of questioning. Other areas have a similar tone to the Press Complaints Commission's Code. In dealing with children, the right to privacy is a prime concern, together with the need for permission from a parent or those *in loco parentis* to film or record the child.

As with the Press Complaints Commission, the BSC will not consider a complaint if a legal action has been started or if there is a legal remedy available. The Commission may adjudicate on the matter without a hearing or require you to attend a hearing at the Commission's offices. If the complaint is upheld in full or partially, the Commission can tell the broadcaster to publish a summary of your complaint together with the Commission's findings.

One quirk is that, although the BSC has been set up by statute to oversee the broadcasters, it has no right to order an apology or correction nor to make an award for financial compensation.

The Independent Television Commission

The Independent Television Commission (ITC) is the programme regulator for the ITV contractors (Channel 3), Channel 4 and Channel 5. It does not cover the Welsh fourth channel, S4C (http://www.s4c.co.uk), which has its own regulatory authority.

The ITC programme code contains a specific section on privacy which, as with the previous two bodies, sets out what is and is not acceptable. By and large, the tone and content is the same. The ITC (http://itc.org.uk) has a broader remit than pursuing individual complaints. It was set up to award licences to broadcast contractors, to monitor performance against the terms of a licence and to ensure fair and effective competition in the provision of the services. In fairness, the investigation of complaints and publication of the findings is also contained in the ITC's brief, but the body's role is much broader than the organizations mentioned so far.

The ITC recommends that issues be taken up directly with the television company concerned. As before, you need to have full details of the item concerned and reasons for your complaint.

The Radio Authority

The Radio Authority (RA) was created by the Broadcasting Act of 1990, which split radio and television from the former Independent Broadcasting Authority. The RA deals with the licensing and regulation of commercial radio within the UK, and so performs a similar task for radio as the ITC does for television. Stations must not broadcast material which is unfair, inaccurate or likely to cause widespread offence. The Authority carries out part of its regulatory duty by acting on complaints from listeners.

The RA also recommends that people with a complaint about a programme should first write to the station concerned and then take it up with the Authority if they are not satisfied. There is a complaints form contained on the RA website (http://www.radioauthority.org.uk) which can be downloaded. The complaint needs to be filed within 42 days of the broadcast. If the Authority believes there is a prima facie case of one of their Codes having been broken, tapes of the broadcast and/or scripts will be requested and examined. The radio station is also sent a copy of the person's complaint for comment.

The Authority makes public a summary of upheld complaints, and can impose sanctions on the radio station ranging from an advisory note to a revocation of the station's right to broadcast (this latter point, at least, in theory).

The British Broadcasting Corporation

The BBC provides television, radio and teletext services throughout the UK. A broadcast organization so vast needs a consistent programming framework to work within. This comes through the 'Producers' Guidelines', which run into dozens of pages and are statements of good practice which are expected to be adhered to throughout the Corporation. Producers' Guidelines, available on the Internet (http://www.bbc.co.uk/info/editorial/prodgl), cover most eventualities that broadcasters are likely to come across.

They are comprehensive and are the rulebook against which programmes can be judged. The Guidelines contain a full chapter (chapter 6) on how BBC producers are to handle recordings with children.

If you have a complaint against a broadcast by the BBC, there are a number of ways in which to complain or comment. If you are dealing with a local radio or regional television station, you can contact the programme producer direct and progress through the hierarchy there. The Producers' Guidelines will generally be used as a basis for consideration of the complaint. The BBC also has a national feedback and inquiry line which logs complaints and comments to pass to individual producers (0870-010-0222). This is particularly appropriate for a broadcast on one of the national radio or television channels. If you are making a specific complaint which requires a response, this needs to be made clear and possibly followed up in writing. The BBC has a Programme Complaints Unit (PCU) for serious complaints.

While the complaints procedure mentioned in this section is contained within the BBC, the opportunity of submitting a complaint to the Broadcasting Standards Council is also available.

The aim of this book is to help you work towards a more profitable relationship with the people who make the news – the media. Its intention is not just to help you think of ways of getting your school into the press and on air but also to change people's perceptions of your school for the better. We cannot stress too much the need to strike up good professional ties with the education correspondent or a journalist from the local newspaper and radio station.

Chapter 9

Sharing the vision

Making public relations and media relations
part of a whole school policy.

In this book, we have considered the practical issues that schools should deal with in communicating effectively. But we believe that schools have a duty to communicate effectively with the public. We have seen how the predominant culture within education has changed over the past fifteen years or so, and how schools are – rightly in our view – less isolated from, and more accountable to, their communities.

In 1963, the Newsom Report on secondary education (DES, 1963) suggested that a school should be joined to its community by 'a causeway well trodden in both directions'. This 'St Michael's Mount' view of the school is no longer appropriate or acceptable. Schools have to reflect the current legislation on management, governance and accountability, by being an integral part of the community they serve.

What community?

The governing body and staff of the school must have a clear idea of who constitutes the school community. Is it purely a geographical community, where the school serves a discrete neighbourhood? This is becoming less common. More likely, there will be a number of neighbourhoods and communities served by the school. Some may be unremittingly suburban and comparatively homogenous. Others will be inner-city – part regenerated and part traditional. The range of wealth and poverty served by the school may come close to mirroring the extraordinary diversity of the national population. Elsewhere, schools will serve large rural areas of small towns, villages, hamlets and isolated settlements – again encompassing huge ranges of wealth and cultural experience. Each will have different demands and needs in terms of style and purpose of communication. Many schools nowadays serve a religious (or at least quasi-religious) community. Aided and foundation Church schools may be able to set very clear criteria on admissions; controlled Church schools will retain some religious ethos, while needing to recognize the rights of non-Church members. Many otherwise open-enrolment schools now select some of their pupils by 'aptitude'. Other schools will serve very loose and widely flung communities. Certain schools in inner-city London, for example, define their catchment as being within the M25. Other schools serve 'communities' of disability, where the only things held in common by pupils are more or less loosely defined learning difficulties.

It would be a nonsense to expect each of these schools to have identical styles and means of communicating with their public. In each case, of course, the school must first define its public. This will include not just pupils and parents, but also neighbours, prospective pupils and parents, other catchment schools, local councillors and education officers, staff elsewhere, as well as the entire staff of the school. The characteristics of this public will determine all policies concerned with both internal and external communication.

Whose responsibility?

It is for this reason that the governing body should be the first and major arena for discussion and policy-making. The ultimate responsibility for the conduct of the school lies with its governing body – of whom the headteacher is a key, but not the only, member. The 1998 Education Act requires the governing body 'to conduct the school with a view to promoting high standards'. Governors will delegate some of their functions to committees and individuals. Vitally, the governing body delegates day-to-day management of the school to the headteacher. But the head is required to manage the school in the light of the governing body's broad policies and statements.

So it is the governing body's job to:

- ensure that legal requirements are met in the supply and publication of information to the Secretary of State, the local education authority, the Office for Standards in Inspection and the parents (the DfEE Guide to the Law gives full information on what is required);

- meet its moral responsibilities in ensuring that parents and the community are given real opportunities to participate in the life of the school, to challenge its performance and to support their children as partners in learning;
- go further than legal requirements to ensure that the school publishes – in such a way as to encourage challenge and participation – minutes of all its non-confidential procedures, all its policies and procedures (in accessible formats), its standards, achievements and targets;
- make the school genuinely accessible and welcoming to parents in a structured – preferably negotiated – way;
- share its messages, its meanings, its aspirations with all its publics.

The governing body establishes and leads the culture of the school, most notably in the staff it employs and in the vision of the school it promotes in its strategic plan. Determining the direction of the school entails setting aims, objectives, principles and targets for the school (see Gann, 1998). The governors then devise policies and procedures that provide the framework within which the staff work to achieve those aims. The governing body then ensures that its plans are being achieved by continuous monitoring and evaluation of their policies and procedures.

It will do this through the work done by committees, whose major task it is to oversee the effectiveness of the policies in its areas of responsibility. But it will also ensure that the collective eye of the governing body is kept 'on the ball' by strategies such as an annual review day. This day, which allows governors (and staff and others, where appropriate) to look in detail at what the school has achieved during the past twelve months, and what it will focus on during the coming year, is ideally held in the summer months. It is the centrepiece event of the strategic governing body. From it should emerge a mass of information for communicating to the school's stakeholders: parents, pupils, staff and others.

The annual review

The annual school review by the governing body is an essential tool in the formulation of the school's culture – and therefore of the image which the school chooses to project. Without this, PR policies, marketing strategies and media relations are merely day-to-day tactics. The annual review might have the following as its central agenda, although priorities may change from year to year according to circumstances:

- to confirm and/or amend the school's mission (or vision or aims – whatever language is used for the overall direction of the school);
- to determine a calendar for the review of school policies and procedures throughout the coming year;
- to agree priorities or key issues for the coming year (and beyond, if appropriate);
- to set whole school targets for outcomes (not necessarily the statutory targets for outputs – e.g. test results, which may be reviewed in the autumn).

This gives the governing body the following material to communicate (and to consult on, where appropriate):

- the school vision;
- key policies;
- targets.

A communications strategy

Among the policies needed by a school is a communications strategy (although this might be called a marketing strategy or a public relations policy). Its primary purpose is to optimize the school's presentation of itself to its pupils, parents, staff and other members of the community. Within this communications strategy, there will be a section that deals with the media. It is crucial that within this section the techniques to be used in communicating with the media – whether proactively or reactively – match the beliefs and culture of the school.

An overall strategy will include:

- *Events:* regular parents' evenings explaining the curriculum, behaviour management and other pastoral policies; a support group or parents'/friends' association focusing on raising school performance rather than money; social, educational and cultural events; workshops; governors' and teachers' surgeries; transport and crèches.

- *An annual parents' evening* which addresses the expressed concerns of the parent and student body, organized in such a way and at such a time that the maximum number of parents is involved.
- *Communications:* school, staff and governors' handbooks; information leaflets; curriculum updates (say, half-termly) for each class or subject; school notice-boards; informative assessment and reporting systems; continuous monitoring of all formal and informal school communications with pupils, parents, staff and the wider community, including identification of 'key' community figures; a home-school policy which reflects parental needs as well school demands.
- *A range of extra-curricular events:* clubs, trips, visits, sports – e.g. breakfast club; homework club – meeting the needs of the whole school population.
- *A market research strategy* which regularly and comprehensively provides parental, student, staff and other feedback and raises parental concerns; the strategy must include arrangements for disseminating results and acting on them.
- *A 'parents in school' policy* including volunteer helpers, parent–teacher projects, resources for parents.
- *A school access policy* which provides clear and simple arrangements for parental visits and access to staff; home visits; an induction programme; a policy of community use which is aimed at raising the profile of the school as a community facility, not at earning profits.
- *A policy for reception,* including staffing of the school office; arrangements for two-way emergency telephone contact; clear and appropriate signing around the school; an appropriate balance of welcoming open access with effective security.
- *Regular opportunities for staff in-service training* in all the above.

For further help in these strategies, we recommend Waller and Waller (1998), Capper *et al.* (1998) and Gann (1999).

And finally . . .

No single part of the school's practice can be treated as isolated from its values, its beliefs and its image. Governing bodies will want to promote high standards in *all* areas of the school's practice. The school's public profile tells its public the kind of school it is, its aspirations for its children, the messages that are given out day by day, by default as much as by intention.

All schools now are 'in the spotlight' – continuously, incessantly. Although this increases the stress on staff and on children, it is the necessary corollary of education being valued and being talked about now more than at any time in the past hundred years.

Being in the spotlight brings rewards, provided it is seen as part of the school's mission to communicate to, to enlist and to share its learning with its public.

Appendix I
Case studies

Each of these case studies is adapted from a real event which took place in a school within the past ten years. Only the names have been changed. Each case can be used to illustrate how either a sudden or a developing crisis might be handled by the governing body to enable either damage limitation or actual benefit to be gained. All the cases are reactive. Responses would take place within the framework of an established communications policy.

Case study 1

Case study 1

Arsonists hit school

ARSONISTS were today blamed for a £70,000 blaze at a Charston school which destroyed two classrooms and sent pupils' work up in flames.

The fire broke out today at Purston Boys School shortly before 5 a.m. after five classrooms were broke into.

A wooden prefabricated building was destroyed and at least 50 windows cracked or smashed.

Staff contacted exam boards to find out what could be done if any exam work had been lost.

Headteacher Christopher Peters said: 'We don't know if there was any year ten course work in there and staff that teach in those rooms are very upset.

'It looks almost certain it was arson because there were signs of an attempt to light a fire in two other rooms.'

continued on next page

Case study 1 continued

Five classes have now squeezed into alternative rooms but lessons were not disrupted.

Exams taking place this morning went ahead as normal and Mr Peters said staff had responded magnificently.

Fire crews were alerted by a school neighbour but could only stop the blaze spreading. Hightown firefighter Colin Lee said: 'You could see the flames from Hurley Road. It had probably been going quite a while when we got there. It was burned to the ground.'

City council surveyors were on site this morning to start the clear-up.

'It was an elderly temporary classroom made of wood and it went up like tinder,' said Mr Peters. 'When I got there, it was very smoky and now there are only one or two pieces left.

'Windows in the hall and kitchen are cracked but there is no immediate danger.

'I am furious that such a thing could happen and, apparently, so easily. If it is arson, it is absolutely appalling.'

Arsonists hit school

1   What action should the governing body take on the morning after the fire?

2   What communications from the school might a parent want to see directly from the school immediately after the fire? What about over the following weeks?

3   What image of the school is projected by the photograph? What image is projected by the headteacher's remarks?

4   What *answers* does the newspaper article provide to pupils? To parents? To staff? To the wider community?

Case study 2

School bullies held in dawn raids

A SCHOOL bullying ring blamed for robbing, beating and blackmailing children has been smashed in a series of dawn police raids.

Victims have been terrorized for eight months but had been silenced by fear.

The scale of the racket was uncovered only after a surveillance operation and hours of questioning by detectives.

Last night ten boys between 13 and 15 were facing 35 charges and will appear in juvenile court next month.

The school involved is a comprehensive in Charbridge. But Detective Inspector William Mulcaster, who led the investigation, said: 'This could be happening in any playground in the country. We are talking of a well-respected school where children have been striking terror into fellow pupils day after day.

'There have been beatings and blackmail. Some of the children have been going hungry because all their dinner money has been stolen. They've been too frightened to tell their parents.

'Some have been bed-wetting, others faltering in their lessons and turning moody at home. Some had simply been staying away from school.'

The first clue surfaced in February when the parents of a 13-year-old boy called police with suspicions that he was being bullied.

A woman officer went to their home to interview the boy, and, said Mr Mulcaster, sensed from his replies that there was a deeper problem.

A small squad of officers was installed at a local police station and, in conjunction with school staff, launched an investigation which was to last three months.

Officers in plain clothes kept watch on the school and the surrounding streets. Hundreds of questionnaires were sent to parents asking them to sit down with their children and ask them if they had had money taken from them, had been assaulted or threatened, or knew of other victims.

The same names began to emerge and the horror stories dated back to September.

Large numbers had been extorted out of their pocket and dinner money. Those who resisted were beaten up.

Police discreetly visited the homes of the victims and took lengthy statements as parents listened in horror. Early on Wednesday, officers

continued on next page

Case study 2 continued

arrived simultaneously at nine homes in the town's St James' Park, Horton Street and Forde areas. The ten, including two brothers, were taken in for questioning.

Constable Liz Moore, one of the officers involved, said: 'This was not normal playground bullying. It was extortion, blackmail and assault.'

Mr Mulcaster said: 'The one complaint was the tip of a dreadful iceberg. We have 25 witnesses who we hope will give evidence, but they are just the worst affected. There are many more.

'We have to take advice from the Crown Prosecution Serive on how we proceed. These boys are deeply distressed and concerned about the consequences of appearing in court. Their well-being is a major consideration.

'We are frankly horrified by what we found. But this is not unique. The message is: all parents, all schools, take heed.

'Be on the lookout for bruising, children going quiet, moodiness. It may not be down simply to adolescence.'

The headmaster of the 1,000-pupil mixed-sex school, said: 'We hope the actions taken will serve as a message to all school bullies. It is something that will be eradicated.'

School bullies held in dawn raids

1 What image of the school is projected by this story? What might we infer about the headteacher? the staff? the governing body?
2 What action might have been taken between February (when the police learned of the incidents) and May (when the story was published) to forestall some of the impact?
3 What might a press release look like on the day when the story broke?

Case study 3

Pupils spy teachers naked in classroom sex romp

PUPILS who peeped into a classroom found two teachers in the middle of a naked sex romp.

The couple had locked themselves in but did not realize there was a gap at one window, where children spied on them.

The teachers, both married, but not to each other, were suspended pending an emergency governors' meeting tonight at Berry Court High School in Burwick.

One 15-year-old pupil said: 'The two teachers had locked themselves in a classroom and were completely naked.

'They thought nobody could see them, but some third and fourth year pupils were peeping. They saw them having sex.'

Stupid

School governor Audrey Black said: 'How those teachers could be so stupid I just don't know. I can scarcely believe that anything like this could happen in school. I was amazed when I found out the reasons for a special meeting.'

Derek Book, chairman of the governors, said he was not aware of any reaction from parents. He added: 'There has been an alleged incident involving two members of staff. The headmaster has looked into the matter and has satisfied himself that there are grounds for investigation. The teachers have been relieved of their duties until further notice.'

The staff members involved were not identified and the man believed to have been involved refused to comment yesterday.

His two children were taken out for the day by a friend, leaving him and his wife alone to discuss their problems.

Pupils spy teachers naked in classroom sex romp

Any governing body's nightmare!

1 How might the chair of governors best deal with the media interest? Propose a strategy.
2 Which quotes in the story are helpful to the school? Which are unhelpful? What policy or guidelines might have prevented the least helpful?
3 On the limited evidence of the story, what action might the governing body and headteacher take now? What might they announce? What media, if any, might they use to announce it?
4 What information should now be given to the pupils? To the parents?

Case study 4

Boy, 6, stranded by teachers on seaside trip

Mum slams school over ordeal

A BOY aged 6 was left stranded on a beach 90 miles from home when teachers forgot him after a school outing.

Kevin Moor was found wandering alone wearing just a pair of shorts 90 minutes after his classmates left the seaside.

He was only reported missing when mum Tracy, 31, of Oldley arrived at school to collect him after coaches returned from Skegness.

Staff from St Saviour C of E primary rang Skegness police, who confirmed they had Kevin. A couple had found him on the beach.

The youngster was reunited with his mum after two teachers drove Tracy to the coast.

Last night Tracy, who is considering legal action, said: 'How could teachers have been so irresponsible? When I realized he was missing I got into a state. He could have been washed out to sea, run down by a bus – anything.'

'I was so relieved to see him. I just smothered him with kisses.'

Dad Richard, 30, added: 'It's lucky he wasn't found by some pervert. You'd think teachers would do a head count. We've yet to receive an explanation.'

Kevin said: 'I enjoyed it at first, building sandcastles, then I got hungry and scared.'

The local council said a full investigation had been launched and the school was reviewing its procedures.

Boy, 6, stranded by teachers on seaside trip

Every teacher's nightmare!

1 What is the effect of the absence of any comment from the school?
2 What might any comment or press release say?
3 What action, statements or policies might be introduced by the governing body to ensure that there is no repetition of this incident? How might parents be mollified?

Case study 5

Clocked car headmaster faces action

A COUNTY school headmaster faces possible disciplinary action after being fined £700 for 'clocking' a car.

Educational chiefs and school governors will hold talks after last week's court appearance by Martin Brown, head of Loamshire's Clydestown secondary school.

Mr Brown, who had knocked 60,000 miles off a B-reg Austin Montego's odometer, asked a motor dealer to sell it.

Tom Harcourt, Loamshire's deputy director of education, said a decision on disciplinary action had still to be determined.

He added: 'It's a matter initially for the school governing body. We are in touch with them through the chairman to discuss if any action will be taken.

Chairman Winston Lipscombe said he had spoken to most of the governors. 'They are disappointed this has happened,' he said. 'Our first consideration has to be for the school. Nobody has been in touch with me to express horror or dissatisfaction.'

Mr Brown appeared before Cordleton magistrates on August 24th after being investigated by the county trading standards department. He became head of the school in 1987.

Clocked car headmaster faces action

1 Given that charges would have been laid some months before this court appearance, what action might the governors have taken earlier?
2 What might a press release from the chair of governors say?
3 Given the recent history of the school (see the last paragraph), what effect might this news story have on the pupils and parents of the school? What can the governing body do to allay their fears?

Case study 6

Readers write:

I am feeling angry and frustrated at being faced with a wall of silence.

Several months ago, the headteacher of my son's school announced, with apparent pride, that the school had entered a sponsorship agreement with a local manufacturer in the aerospace business.

Only a few weeks earlier, I had been among the protesters outside our nearest Crown Court. This was during the trial of four women activists who broke into the company's plant and took hammers to an aircraft destined for East Timor – one of 24 similar aircraft due for export to the military government in Indonesia. The women, part of the Swords into Ploughshares campaign, were acquitted after they defended themselves against a charge of causing £500,000 worth of damage, claiming they were trying to prevent the greater crime of assisting genocide.

On receiving the news of the sponsorship, I published a letter in both of our local newspapers, recounting my disgust at the school's behaviour. Not one reply, either way, was published and the school has maintained a total silence, refusing to respond in any way.

Subsequently, a director of the company was the guest speaker at a school prize-giving.

My objections have been treated with amused contempt, and I am regarded as an unbalanced eccentric. What am I to do? Stage a one-man violent protest?

Next week

This is an extract from a readers' advice column.

1   Consider the competing interests in this story. What publicity strategy, developed before the initial announcement, might the governing body have adopted to see them through this sponsorship agreement?

Appendix 2
School inspection

The governing body has a number of statutory duties connected with OfSTED's regular (normally, six-yearly) inspection of the school. Specifically, it has to:

- comment on the inspection job to be done;
- notify parents and others of inspection;
- arrange a meeting between the registered inspector and parents;
- provide information to the registered inspector;
- distribute the inspection report and summary;
- draw up an action plan;
- inform parents in the annual report about follow-up of the action plan.

(Department for Education and Employment, *A Guide to the Law for School Governors*, DfEE, 2000)

The way these matters are handled is of crucial importance. The regular formal school inspection is the only statutory event designed to inform the public about how well the school is doing. Of course, it makes formal judgements about those things which OfSTED and the DfEE consider important. So, while the governors are obliged to publish OfSTED's opinions, there is nothing to stop them deciding – as far as they are allowed to – the context of the reporting. How might the parents' meeting with the registered inspector be presented? Does it have to be a formal event with parents sitting in rows? Or is it worth talking to the inspector about another format with which your parents are likely to be more comfortable? Is it possible to help parents feel that they at least share in the ownership of the process?

What should be published to the parents about the inspection before it happens? How might they contribute? What should pupils be told – and when? There is evidence that some children feel the stress of inspection – clearly, staff do. How can this best be handled?

What information should be given to the inspection team? They will make it clear what they want, but this does not stop you giving them more – whatever you think may be useful in helping them to reach an accurate judgement on what *you* think is important about your school and its achievements.

After the inspection, the governing body is required to distribute the summary report. How you do this is important. Some schools have found that the summary report (Section 1 of the full version) does not by itself fairly reflect the full report. In this case, schools have felt it worthwhile to incur the extra expense of distributing the full version.

Certainly, when you release it to the press, as you must do, you will want to put the report into context. This may be an accessible version written by yourselves. It might take the form of a summary of the action plan, focusing less on 'what is wrong' and more on 'what we are going to do about it'. Preferably, it will say, 'This is what we are *already* doing about it.'

The examples given here show that, for many people, whether the report itself is positive or negative is less important than what the local press says about it. You may not have much power over OfSTED but, as we have seen, you have some influence over the press.

Example 1 headlines a serious criticism, although some positive comments are reported. The school in Example 2 has taken matters into its own hands. While the local paper will report the school inspection in its own way, its advertising department is happy to publish (at some price, of course) the school's own spin on it. Elsewhere, Examples 3 and 4 show how a positive headline is extracted from a not entirely favourable report. Perhaps the block advertisement the school took out for the same day had some influence on this?

When the news is more serious – where a school is designated as failing its pupils, for example – the news release will tell the truth, but then focus on the steps that are already being taken to put things right. Following this, make sure that people – pupils, parents and the wider community – are kept in touch with all the progress that is being made.

All the stories that appear about schools are only part of a larger story: the story of the school itself. This is the story that you want people to read.

Example 1

Watchdog criticizes school
by *Express* reporter

TEACHING at Woodberry Infant School, Priesthill, has been severely criticized in an OfSTED report for creating under-achievers.

Many youngsters behave poorly and lack concentration because teachers are not tailoring lessons to their abilities, government inspectors state.

Teachers are criticized for having 'significant weaknesses' in some subject knowledge and many need more training.

Inspectors acknowledge that the school, which changed from being part of a First to an Infant School last September, is going through a difficult period of transition, but say: 'There are significant shortcomings in important aspects of the education provided for children.'

Pupils beginning at the school reach high reading standards, but the report states: 'Their skills are not developed systematically as they move through the school.'

Inspectors who visited the school in May highlighted teaching to 6- and 7-year-olds as the main area of weakness but say the majority of children achieve national expectations.

Joan Lord, who has headed the school since September, is praised as the school's main asset for tackling the problems.

Miss Lord told the *Express*: 'We lost senior staff in the change and many of my staff had to teach new areas. We will have training for them.'

She added that the school is following a development plan which is leading to improvements, and said: 'We have worked very hard so far and I am confident for the future.'

Example 2

Governors delighted with inspectors' report

Charwood

Pupils at Charwood School receive a good education. The school offers a caring community in which most pupils are helped to achieve their full potential and are well prepared for adult life.

(OfSTED Report, June 1995)

Pupils	Staff and teachers	Parents and community
• The quality of pupils' learning is a particular strength. • Pupils are attentive and work conscientiously at the tasks they are set. • The school values pupils equally and develops sound moral integrity. It is successful in achieving its aims in the context of an orderly, welcoming community. • Pupils' social development is very good.	• The school is generously staffed, resulting in class sizes which are comparatively small. • The work of the teaching staff is a strength of the school. They display a high degree of commitment and professionalism. • Non-teaching staff make an important contribution to the work of the school. • Curriculum provision has a positive impact on quality of experience and standards achieved. This is enhanced by the regular and effective use of homework in most subjects.	• The school community provides an atmosphere of care and consideration. There is particular emphasis on making the school a safe place. • Parents have a high regard for the work of the school.

- Standards achieved by pupils with Special Educational Needs are mainly at a level appropriate to their abilities.
- Year 11 pupils often show a good understanding of their strengths and weaknesses and use this well in planning their revision.
- The school has a quiet, orderly and purposeful atmosphere, and its pupils are generally well behaved in class and around the school and its grounds.
- There is little evidence of bullying, and incidents, however minor, are taken seriously by the school.

- Changes in the recent past have been managed well, and the school has a clear sense of direction expressed by aims, goals and development plan.
- The head and deputy heads give a string lead which has a positive effect on the development of the school.
- The governing body takes its supervisory role seriously.

- Transfer from the two main feeder schools is imaginatively and sensitively handled.
- Arrangements for pupils transferring to the local colleges are managed well.
- The school provides good value for money.

Example 3

Teaching standards win praise from inspectors

TEACHERS at a Southampton school have been given a pat on the back by a team of watchdogs.

OfSTED inspectors who visited Wealdhall Community School in November praised teaching standards and found most pupils were doing well.

The watchdogs found teaching and learning was sound in 80 per cent of the lessons observed at the 578-pupil school.

Although many children failed to meet national standards in most lessons, the inspectors reported they were achieving in line with their abilities.

The OfSTED report noted that the school was in transition after a number of staff changes in the past two years, but stated that initiatives had been taken to solve problems.

The inspectors did, however, make the disturbing observations that a 'significant minority' of pupils behaved badly in lessons, and said there were a small number of children who were repeatedly absent.

Standards of reading and writing were also criticized, and the school was told its religious education, design and technology failed to meet national requirements.

Example 4

Wealdhall Community School

Wealdhall Community School was inspected in November 1995.

What the Inspectors said about us:

'Wealdhall Community School provides a sound education for the majority of its pupils'

- the quality of teaching and learning was sound or better or good, in over 80 per cent of the lessons observed;
- lessons are well planned;
- activities provide appropriate challenges for differing abilities;
- most pupils have a positive attitude to learning; they show interest and a willingness to learn;
- most pupils achieve appropriately in relation to their abilities;
- the school provides sound value for money;
- the behaviour and discipline of the majority of pupils is satisfactory and the school provides a generally orderly community.

'This is a school in transition.'

- new initiatives undertaken to improve aspects of performance are beginning to have a positive impact. Inspectors also said that key aspects of performance require improvement. We are already working on:
- levels of absence and the behaviour of some pupils;
- standards of literacy;
- strategic planning;
- provision for students' spiritual, moral, social and cultural development.

A full Action Plan will be completed by 6 March 1996. In partnership with pupils and parents, we seek success over the coming months.

Please contact us for a copy of the Inspection Report.

Appendix 3
Contact details for
UK media regulatory bodies

Press Complaints Commission
Press Complaints Commission
1 Salisbury Square
London
EC4Y 8JB

Telephone: 020-7353-3732 (0131-222-6652 in Scotland)
Textphone: 020-7583-2264
Fax: 020-7353-8355
e-mail: pcc@pcc.org.uk
Internet: http://www.pcc.org.uk

Broadcasting Standards Commission
Broadcasting Standards Commission
7 The Sanctuary
London
SW1P 3JS

Telephone: 020-7808-1000
Fax: 020-7233-0397
e-mail: bsc@bsc.org.uk
Internet: http://www.bsc.org.uk

Independent Television Commission
Independent Television Commission
33 Foley Street
London
W1W 7TL

Telephone: 020-7255-3000
Fax: 020-7306-7800
Minicom: 020-7306-7753
e-mail: publicaffairs@itc.org.uk
Internet: http://www.itc.org.uk

Radio Authority
Radio Authority
Holbrook House
14 Great Queen Street
Holborn
London
WC2B 5DG

Telephone: 020-7430-2724
Fax: 020-7405-7062
e-mail: reception@radioauthority.org.uk
Internet: http://www.radioauthority.org.uk

British Broadcasting Corporation

BBC	*or*	BBC Programme Information
Broadcasting House		PO Box 1116
London		Belfast
W1A 1AA		BT2 7AJ
		(This section deals with programme inquiries from the whole of the United Kingdom.)

Telephone: 0870-010-0222
Minicom: 0870-010-0212
e-mail: info@bbc.co.uk
Internet: http://www.bbc.co.uk

The addresses and contact details of local and regional BBC stations can be found in the phone book.

Bibliography

Books

Auld, R. (1976) *William Tyndale Junior and Infants Schools Public Inquiry: A Report to the Inner London Education Authority*, London: ILEA.

Bartram, P. (1999) *Writing a Press Release*, Oxford: How To Books.

Berg, L. (1968) *Risinghill: Death of a Comprehensive School*, London: Penguin.

Black, S. (1989) *Introduction to Public Relations*, London: Modino Press.

—— (1993) *The Essentials of Public Relations*, London: Kogan Page.

Capper, L., Downes, P. and Jenkinson, D. (1998) *Successful Schools: Parental Involvement in Secondary Schools*, Coventry: CEDC.

Clark, P. (1998) *Back from the Brink: Transforming the Ridings School – and our Children's Education*, London: Metro Books.

Cullen, Lord (1996) *The Public Inquiry into the Shootings at Dunblane Primary School on 13 March 1996*, Edinburgh: The Stationery Office.

Daily Telegraph (1972) 'Sauce for the Goose', London: *Daily Telegraph* leader, 28 September 1972.

Department for Education and Employment (DfEE) (2000a) *A Guide to the Law for School Governors, January 2000*, London: DfEE.

—— (2000b) *New Regulations and Guidance on the Roles of Governing Bodies and Headteachers*, London: DfEE.

Department of Education and Science (DES) (1963) *Half our Future, A Report of the Central Advisory Council for Education (The Newsom Report)*, London: HMSO.

—— (1977) *Education in Schools: A Consultative Document*, London: HMSO.

Fletcher, C. *et al.* (1985) *Schools on Trial*, Milton Keynes: Open University Press.

Gann, N. (1998) *Improving School Governance: How Better Governors Make Better Schools*, London: Falmer Press.

—— (1999) *Targets for Tomorrow's Schools: A Guide to Whole School Target-setting for Governors and Headteachers*, London: Falmer Press.

Grace, G. (1972) *Role Conflict and the Teacher*, London: Routledge & Kegan Paul.

Harrison, S. (1995) *Public Relations*, London: Routledge.

Haywood, R. (1991) *All about Public Relations*, Maidenhead: McGraw-Hill.

HMSO (1986), *Education No. 2 Act 1986*, London: HMSO.

Johnson, G. and Scholes, K. (1999) *Exploring Corporate Strategy* (5th edn), London: Prentice Hall.

Macpherson, M. (1972) 'The school parents didn't want', London: *Evening Standard*, 5 December 1972.

Riley, K. (1998) *Whose School is it Anyway?* London: Falmer Press.

Stirling Council Education Services (1999) *Should Crisis Call: Crisis Management in Schools, Effective Preparation and Response*, Stirling Council.

Stone, N. (1995) *The Management and Practice of Public Relations*, Basingstoke: Macmillan.

Strong, E. (1925) *The Psychology of Selling*, New York: McGraw-Hill.

Van Riel, C.B.M. (1995) *Principles of Corporate Communication*, Hemel Hempstead: Prentice Hall.

Waller, H. and Waller, J. (1998) *Linking Home and School: Partnership in Practice in Primary Education*, London: David Fulton.

Wilby, P. (1976) 'School's better now, OK?', London: *Observer*, 1 February 1976.

Yule, W. and Gold, A. (1993) *Wise before the Event: Coping with Crises in School*, London: Calouste Gulbenkian Foundation.

Websites

British Broadcasting Corporation   http://www.bbc.co.uk
Broadcasting Standards Commission   http://www.bsc.org.uk
Independent Television Commission   http://www.itc.org.uk
Press Complaints Commission   http://www.pcc.org.uk
Radio Authority   http://www.radioauthority.org.uk
S4C   http://www.s4c.co.uk

Interactive Media Software

Media Control (2000) from   http://www.mediacontrol.co.uk

Index